THE COMPLEAT ANGLER'S WIFE

SUZANNE BEEDELL

THE COMPLEAT ANGLER'S WIFE

A complete guide to cooking the angler's catch

COUNTRYWISE BOOKS

THE COMPLEAT ANGLER'S WIFE

is published by

Countrywise Books: The Farmers Weekly

161/166 Fleet Street, London EC4

is made and printed in Great Britain by

William Clowes and Sons, Limited

London and Beccles

and is designed by

Don Marshall

©

National Trade Press Limited

1964

COUNTRYWISE BOOKS

ARE EDITED BY

BARBARA HARGREAVES

✳

Sole Distributors

Temple Press Books

CONTENTS

[5]

[6]

[7]

INTRODUCTION

There are 30,000 species of true fish to be found in the waters of the earth, and fish are a very important item of diet everywhere. This book is concerned with the cooking of the fish which can be caught in the seas and rivers and lakes of our own islands, and the crabs and lobsters, cockles and other shellfish which can be caught in the rocks and mudflats around our coasts.

From the fighting salmon and trout, caught with expensive tackle and much skill, in water costing £1000 a mile, to the little tench pulled out of a flooded gravel pit more by luck than judgement by a ten-year-old boy, there isn't a fish that cannot be made delicious or disgusting by the way it is cooked. It is up to us, fishing wives and fishing mothers, to know how to cope with the piscatorial offerings of our menfolk. Although the greater part of the pleasure for them is in the catching, and although nowadays most coarse fish are weighed and measured and put back, and only the occasional foul hooked specimen is brought home, the edibility of the catch does justify the time and money spent! Well-cooked fish can be a "gastronomic experience".

"Sometimes I have seen slovenly scullions abuse good fish most grossly."
THOMAS BARKER, 1657

[9]

How to Prepare Fish

Fish for cooking must always be fresh, but this should be no problem for the fisherman's wife.

CLEANING FISH   Flat fish are cleaned by cutting out the gills, then making a small incision in the stomach, just behind the head, and pulling out the gut. Wash the fish well and, if required, remove the head with a semi-circular cut.

Round fish are cleaned by slitting the stomach from the head towards the tail, and removing the entrails. Wash well and remove the head with a straight cut if required.

SCALING FISH   With the back of a knife, or with a blunt knife, scrape off the scale, working from tail to head.

[11]

WASHING FISH Always wash fish out with cold, strongly salted water, and never soak fish in unsalted water.

SKINNING FISH Sole should be washed and dried and the fins removed. With the tail facing you cut the skin across just above the tail. Dip your fingers in salt which will help you to grip; then, holding the tail with one hand and the skin with the other, pull the skin hard and quickly towards the head. Other flat fish are skinned after filleting. Lay the fillet down and cut through the flesh only, at the tail end, then work the knife up towards the head, pulling the fillet towards you as you cut.

SPLITTING FISH Having slit the fish and cleaned it, and removed any roe, place on a board cut side down. Then press the fish firmly down with your hand all along the backbone. This will then come away from the flesh easily.

FILLETING FISH Flat fish are filleted thus: Lay the fish on a board and with a sharp pointed knife cut each side of the backbone from head to tail, down to the bone. Start with the left-hand top fillet, and keeping the knife oblique slide it through resting on the bone, taking three or four strokes from head to tail. Pull the fillet off, turn the fish round and repeat, working from tail to head. Turn the fish over and repeat the operation, producing in all four fillets.

Round fish are filleted by placing on a board with the head away from you. With the sharp pointed knife, slit the fish from head to tail, down the backbone. Cut the fillet at the head, and remove. Repeat on the other side, producing in all two fillets.

TRUSSING FISH Whiting are skinned and the tail is drawn through the mouth. Pin the fish thus by passing a skewer through the top of the head, through the tail, and out through the lower jaw. Large Haddock can be trussed in an S shape by passing a long skewer through the centre of the head, through the middle of the body, and through again just above the tail. Tie a piece of tape at each end of the skewer to keep the fish in good shape.

"Good cooks and good fish seldom dwell together."

FRANCK

Cooking Methods

Any of the following methods may be adapted for your particular purpose.

POACHING   If you have a fish kettle it is perfect for poaching fish, but fish can be poached in the oven in a fireproof dish. A fish kettle has a perforated plate in the bottom on which the fish rests and with which it can be lifted out and drained without damage. If you have no fish kettle, whole fish can be handled gently and safely by placing a saucer in the bottom of your stewpan and laying a clean cloth on top with the ends hanging out, making a kind of hammock in which the fish can be slung and lifted out when done.

When cooking trout or salmon a court bouillon (see page 15) is usually prepared first and, when cool, is poured over the fish already in the kettle or pan, never more than just covering the fish. The kettle is placed on a low flame and

[13]

gradually brought up to simmering point, and cooking is carried out very carefully and quietly indeed. If the fish is to be served cold, let it cool in the kettle before draining.

Coarse-fleshed fish cooked in this way (cod, bream, turbot, etc.) should be placed in just boiling court bouillon. This seals the fish at once and keeps in the flavour.

Times for poaching vary with the fish, but fish is done when it goes opaque and exudes a creamy liquid.

When using a fireproof dish for poaching the dish is well buttered and the fish laid in it just covered with court bouillon, and then covered with buttered greaseproof, or with aluminium foil, or its own lid.

FRYING FISH Deep frying is best done in a proper fish fryer with a wire basket, using pure lard. Shallow frying is best done in an ordinary frying pan, in oil or butter. Fish for frying is always coated in some way; either with seasoned flour, batter, or egg and oil and white breadcrumbs. The cleaned, washed, and dried fish should be seasoned with salt and pepper and a little lemon juice, and then dipped in the coating. Test deep fat by dropping in a small piece of bread; if the bread immediately goes crisp and golden the fat is hot enough. If there is no bubbling, heat the fat some more.

Egg and breadcrumb coating is done successfully by beating up egg lightly with a tablespoonful of oil, and seasoning. Put this mixture into a shallow dish and dip the fish into it. Make breadcrumbs by passing stale bread through a coarse sieve. Dip the fish coated with egg mixture into the breadcrumbs, or press the crumbs on with a flat knife. Don't have the fish too wet with egg, nor leave it to soak in the egg; and shake off surplus crumbs before frying.

Fish fried in shallow fat is usually just dipped in seasoned flour. A teaspoonful of curry powder added to the flour will give an unusual taste.

Batter is best made by putting 4 oz. flour, $\frac{1}{4}$ teaspoonful of salt, and an egg into a bowl, and mixing it to a smooth batter with about $\frac{1}{4}$ pint of milk or water. The fish is dipped into this and dropped immediately into hot fat, without a frying basket.

Some fish such as herrings, mackerel, and sprats, which are naturally oily, are dry fried, by being cooked gently in a frying pan without adding extra fat.

STEAMED FISH Wrap the fish in greaseproof paper after sprinkling it with salt, pepper, and lemon juice. Place it in a steamer and cook for 20 minutes to each pound, and 20 minutes extra for large fish.

GRILLING FISH Thick fish should be scored before grilling, and mackerel and herring split open and grilled open side first. Always preheat the grill and brush over both fish and grill with melted butter before cooking.

BAKING FISH Fish should be baked in a fireproof dish with knobs of butter on the fish, according to the various recipes.

Court Bouillon

Court bouillon should always be prepared before fish is cooked. To add the ingredients to the water in which your fish is cooking does not have the same effect at all.

Equal parts of water and white wine.	Small piece of celery.
1 onion.	Salt and peppercorns.
1 clove garlic.	A bouquet garni.
1 carrot.	2 shallots.
	1 clove.

[15]

The water and wine are brought to the boil, and a table-spoonful of vinegar is added to every quart of water. Add all the other ingredients and simmer for an hour.

Court bouillon can be made with the wine omitted.

After using, the court bouillon is often used as the basis of a sauce, or it makes very good fish soup. For this purpose it should be strained, and reheated with the addition of macaroni, spaghetti, or vermicelli, and some grated cheese added just before serving.

The Angler

"He at the least hath his wholesome walk and merry at his ease, a sweet air of the sweet savour of the mead flowers; that maketh him hungry. He heareth the melodious harmony of fowls. He seeth the young swans, herons, ducks, coots, and many other fowl with their broods; which me seemeth better than all the noise of hounds, the blasts of horns, and the cry of fowls; than hunters, falconers, and fowlers can make. And if the angler take fish, surely then there is no man merrier than he in his spirit. Also, whoso will use the game of Angling, he must rise early, which thing is profitable to man in this wise, that is to wit, most to the heal of his soul. For it shall cause him to be holy; and to the heal of his body for it shall cause him to be whole. Also to the increase of his goods, for it shall make him rich."

CHAPTER ONE

SALMON
CHAR
GRAYLING
TROUT
SALMON TROUT

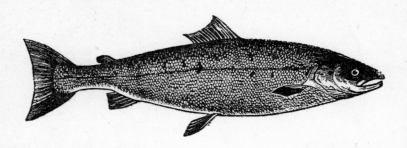

Salmon

"On a blank day one can think about fishing. My mind keeps going back to the people who talk about patience. Put it like this. A man who is fishing for salmon has a whippy piece of wood, attached to the end of which there is a bit of string perhaps as long as a cricket pitch. He has got to wave his piece of wood in such a way as to extend the string behind him, and then drop it in front of him in an absolutely straight line. Many people have difficulty in managing a crop, whose lash is only about four feet long. He repeats this delicate feat perhaps seven hundred times a day, speculating every time about the exact place where he wants the string to land, and he is content to do this for three days running without killing a fish, provided that he kills one on the fourth. This looks to me like a good tribute to the excitement of the kill.

"People seem to think that a fisherman sits in the shade of a pollard willow watching his float, whilst the countryside

[20]

dreams about him, the cuckoo sings, and the cattle draw the grass. It has snowed or sleeted almost every day that I have been here. I have walked perhaps ten miles a day, and been at it nearly twelve hours a day, in the sleet. This is not because I am tough or obstinate but because the joys are so Thrilling (a queer word to use about an art that has nothing to do with steeplechases or motor racing) that it would be unthinkable to do anything else. The fisherman fishes as the urchin eats a cream bun, from lust. You might as well talk about the patience of Tarquin."

"ENGLAND HAVE MY BONES" T. H. WHITE

Boiled Salmon

Scale, clean, and wipe the fish, and cook in plain salted water. Allow 10 minutes per pound, and simmer the fish very gently. Slices of lemon, without peel or pips, can be added to the water while cooking if liked.

Poached Salmon

Place the scaled and cleaned fish in a fish kettle and just cover with cold court bouillon. Bring to simmering point and cook very gently, allowing 10 minutes per pound. Drain and serve hot, or if to be eaten cold, allow to cool in the bouillon.

Both boiled and poached salmon may be served hot with Sauce Bearnaise, or Sauce Hollandaise, or served cold with Sauce Mayonnaise (see Chapter 7).

Baked Salmon New Orleans

2 lb. salmon.

1 teaspoonful sugar.

Pinch of salt and pepper.

1 clove of garlic.

1 red chillie pod
   (or less if not liked too hot).

1 onion.

$\frac{1}{2}$ cup olive oil.

1 tablespoonful
   Worcestershire sauce.

1 tablespoonful vinegar.

2 cupfuls uncooked
   diced potatoes.

3 oz. mushrooms.

$2\frac{1}{2}$ cups cooked tomatoes.

Sprinkle the cleaned salmon with salt and pepper, and put the garlic and chillie inside it. Mince the onion. Brown the sugar in a pan and lay the salmon in it with the onions. Cover with the tomatoes and all ingredients except the mushrooms. Bake in a hot oven for 15 minutes, then add the mushrooms and bake again until the fish is tender.

CULINARY ARTS INSTITUTE ENCYCLOPEDIC COOKBOOK
C.A.L. Chicago

Char

Char is in season in June and July. The flesh is flaky and orange coloured. Any recipe for trout can also be used for char.

Char à la Creme

The fish.	Cup of fresh cream.
Milk.	1 clove of garlic.
Flour.	Chopped parsley.
Butter.	Slices of lemon.

Salt and pepper.

Clean the fish and remove head and fins. Dip in milk and flour, and fry in butter. Put on a plate and season with salt and pepper. Add to the remaining butter in the pan a cup of fresh cream, the crushed garlic and the parsley, beat all well together and heat. Pour the sauce over the fish and serve with slices of lemon.

"LA PÊCHE ET LES POISSONS DE RIVIÈRE" MICHEL DUBORGEL
Libraire Hachette

Grayling

"Umbar or grayling is an amorous fish, that loves a frolic as he loves his life, whose teeth water after every wasp, as his fins flutter after every fly. Pray, when you fish him, fish him finely, for he loves curiosity, neat and slender tackle; and ladylike, you must touch him gently, for to speak plain English, he is tender about the chaps."

FRANCK

At its best in November, grayling should be eaten very fresh. It has an aroma of water thyme, and this must not be allowed to fade before the fish is cooked. Any recipe for trout will do for grayling.

Buttered Grayling

Clean the fish and remove head and tail. Season inside with salt and pepper and drop into deep fat. Turn once and when the fish is done, remove and drain carefully. The skin should come off quite easily now, and the fish is served with plenty of melted butter.

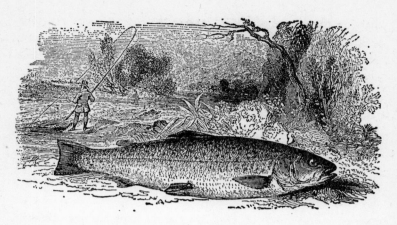

Trout

"The search after food is an instinct belonging to our nature; and from the savage, in his rudest and most primitive state, who destroys a piece of game, or a fish, with a club or a spear, to man in the most cultivated state of society, who employs artifice, machinery, and the resources of various other animals, to secure his object, the origin of the pleasure is similar, and its object the same: but that kind of it requiring the most art may be said to characterise man in his highest intellectual state; and the fisher for salmon and trout with the fly employs not only machinery to assist his physical powers, but applies sagacity to conquer difficulties; and the pleasure derived from ingenious resources and devices, as well as from active pursuit, belongs to this amusement. Then as to its philosophical tendency, it is a pursuit of moral discipline, requiring patience, forbearance, and command of temper. As connected with natural science, it may be vaunted as demanding a knowledge of the habits of a considerable tribe of created beings—fishes, and the animals that they prey upon, and an acquaintance with the signs and tokens of the weather and its

[25]

changes, the nature of waters, and of the atmosphere. As to its poetical relations, it carries us into the most wild and beautiful scenery of nature; amongst the mountain lakes, and the clear and lovely streams that gush from the higher ranges of elevated hills, or that make their way through the cavities of calcareous strata. How delightful in the early spring, after the dull and tedious time of winter, when the frosts disappear and the sunshine warms the earth and waters, to wander forth by some clear stream, to see the leaf bursting from the purple bud, to scent the odours of the bank perfumed by the violet, and enamelled, as it were, with the primrose and the daisy; to wander upon the fresh turf below the shade of the trees, whose bright blossoms are filled with the music of the bee; and on the surface of the waters to view the gaudy flies sparkling like animated gems in the sunbeams, whilst the bright and beautiful trout is watching them from below; to hear the twittering of the water birds, who, alarmed at your approach, rapidly hide themselves beneath the flowers and leaves of the water lily; and as the season advances, to find all these objects changed for others of the same kind, but better and brighter, till the swallow and trout contend, as it were, for the gaudy Mayfly, and till, in pursuing your amusement in the calm and balmy evening, you are serenaded by the songs of the cheerful thrush and melodious nightingale, performing the offices of paternal love, in thickets ornamented with rose and woodbine!''

SIR HUMPHREY DAVY ON ANGLING

"The trout is no single, common, identical, definite, determined and measurable fish, but rather ten thousand tantalising devils."

"THE TARN AND THE LAKE" SIR CHARLES J. HOLMES

THOMAS BARKER'S WAYS TO COOK TROUT

"*Restorative Broth of trouts learn to make;*
Some fry and some stew, and some also bake.
First broyl and then bake is a rule of good skill;
And when thou dost a fortune a great trout to kill
then rost him and bast first with good claret wine:
But the calvor'd boyl'd trout will make thee to dine,
With dainty contentment both the hot and the cold;
And the marrionate trout I dare to be bold,
For a quarter of a year will keep to thy mind,
If covered close and preserved from the wind:
But mark well, good brother, what now I doe say,
Sauce made of anchovies is an excellent way,
With oysters and lemmon, clove nutmeg and mace,
When the brave spotted trout has been boyled apace,
With many sweet herbs; for forty years I,
in Ambassadours kitchins learned my cooker-y
The French and Italian no better can doe;
Observe well my rules and you'll say so too."

BARKER'S DELIGHT, 1657

Always spotted, but varying in colour according to locale, trout makes wonderful eating. There are many recipes, but the fish is so good that the simple ones take a lot of beating.

Very Small Trout Fried

Clean and dry the fish, season inside with salt and pepper, and fry in butter until crisp.

Larger Trout Fried

Larger fish should be cleaned and split. The backbone is

[27]

removed and the fish dipped in oatmeal, fried in dripping, and served with melted butter, or Maître d'Hôtel sauce (see Chapter 7).

Truites au Lard

Fish.	Seasoning.
1 rasher back bacon for each fish.	$\frac{1}{2}$ slice of ham per fish.
	Sliced lemon.
Butter.	Parsley.

Clean and scale the trout. Season and wrap each fish in a rasher of bacon, tying with thread. Put sufficient butter in the pan to fry the fish and place the trout in the hot butter. Cut the ham into strips and put over the fish. Fry on both sides, and serve hot, pouring the juices, the ham and butter from the pan over the fish. Garnish with parsley and lemon slices.

The Irish Ghillies' Way of Baking Trout

All you do is land on a suitable island in an Irish lough—or anywhere else of course—gut and clean your fish quickly in the lake. Meanwhile build a largish wood fire in a hollow scooped in the ground. Make this fire in true pioneer's style so that the best possible draught blows along the trench. Now all you need is a newspaper or two. Wet them in the lake also. When your fire has died down and you have a fair pile of hot ash, wrap your trout individually in wet newspaper having first stuck a nob of butter and some salt inside them. Screw them up tight and bury them in the ashes. When the paper at last begins to smoulder, they should be done.

Delicious. It is rather like tinfoil cooking, all the flavour is trapped inside.

COLIN WILLOCK

[28]

Salmon Trout

Sometimes called the sea trout, this is a migratory trout that lives the greater part of its life in the sea. It is caught in estuaries on its way upriver to breed. "Salmo trutta" is a handsome fish, the male being reddish grey with red spots, and the female steely grey diffused with pink, though, like all trout, the colour and shape may vary slightly according to location. It is in season from March to August, and can be cooked by any of the recipes suitable for trout.

Jellied Salmon Trout

The fish is cleaned and boiled in a fish kettle in salted water. Remove the fish from the kettle very gently as it must be kept whole. When drained lay it in a deep dish and surround it with peeled tomatoes, diced cucumber, and chopped gherkins. Cover the whole with aspic jelly and decorate with cucumber peel. Allow to set.

[29]

Aspic Jelly

1 lb. neck or knuckle of veal.
2½ pints cold water.
Salt.
2 oz. gelatine.
Whites and shells of three eggs.
¼ pint white vinegar.
Bouquet garni.
4 cloves.
10 peppercorns.
Blade of mace.
½ pint white wine.
1 bay leaf.
1 carrot.
½ turnip.
Stick of celery.
1 onion.

Divide the veal and bones and place in salted water. Simmer for 3 hours then strain and allow to cool. Remove all fat and place stock in saucepan with the gelatine. Stand for 20 minutes to soak the gelatine. Whip the egg whites stiffly and add to the stock together with the egg shells which have been washed and crushed. Add all other ingredients except the wine and bring to the boil whisking all the time. Stop whisking and boil for 2 minutes, then move carefully from the stove and allow to settle for 10 minutes. Remove the bouquet garni and add the white wine. Then strain through a jelly bag and the aspic is ready to be poured over the fish.

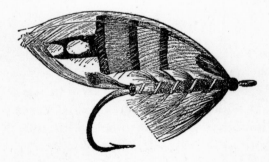

CHAPTER TWO

PIKE	BREAM
RUFFE	TENCH
CARP	BARBEL
PERCH	GUDGEON
ROACH	LOACH
RUDD	BLEAK

BASS

HEAVEN

"Fish (fly replete, in depth of June)
Dawdling away their wat'ry noon)
Ponder deep wisdom, dark or clear,
Each secret fishy hope or fear.
Fish say, they have their Stream and Pond:
But is there anything beyond?
This life cannot be All, they swear,
For how unpleasant, if it were!
One may not doubt that, somehow, Good
Shall come of Water and of Mud:
And, sure, the reverent eye must see
A Purpose in Liquidity.
We darkly know, by Faith we cry,
The future is not Wholly Dry.
Mud unto Mud!—Death eddies near—
Not here the appointed End, not here!
But somewhere, beyond Space and Time,
Is wetter water, slimier slime!
And there (they trust) there swimmeth One
Who swam ere rivers were begun,
Immense, of fishy form and mind,
Squamous, omnipotent, and kind;
And under that Almighty fin,
The littlest fish may enter in.
Oh! never fly conceals a hook,
Fish say, in the Eternal Brook,
But more than mundane weeds are there,
And mud, celestially fair;
Fat caterpillars drift around,
and Paradisal grubs are found;
Unfading moths, immortal flies,
And the worm that never dies.
And in that Heaven of all their wish
There shall be no more land, say fish."

RUPERT BROOKE

[32]

Pike

"There was a Pike taken at Hailbrun, in Swabia, in 1497 with a brazen ring attached to it, on which was inscribed in Greek characters 'I am the fish which was first of all put into the lake by the hands of the governor of the universe, Frederick the Second, the 5th October 1230'. This fish must have been at least two hundred and sixty seven years old, and it is said to have weighed three hundred and fifty pounds."

> *"A slim young pike with smart fins*
> *And grey striped suit, a young cub of a pike*
> *Slouching along away below, half out of sight,*
> *Like a lout on an obscure pavement."*
>
> FROM "FISH" BY D. H. LAWRENCE

Pike with White Wine

The fish.	½ glass white wine.
Chopped onions.	Yolk of one egg.
	3 oz. butter.

Clean the fish and put it in a fireproof dish with the butter and surround with the onions. Pour half a glass of white wine over the fish and cover the dish with aluminium foil. Bake for half an hour in a medium oven. Strain off the liquid and thicken it with the beaten yolk of egg and a little melted butter, and pour over the fish before serving.

Pike with Horseradish Sauce

The fish. 2 oz. butter. Flour. Horseradish.

Clean the Pike but do not scale or remove head. Place the fish in enough lightly salted water to cover it. The fish can be rolled if he is too big for the saucepan. Simmer for twenty minutes. Drain fish, but keep liquor.

Melt the butter in a pan and add a tablespoonful of plain flour, blend, and then add sufficient of the fish liquor to make a sauce the consistency of thin cream, heating gently and stirring all the time. Just before serving, add grated horse-radish to the sauce, but do not cook further. Serve the fish and sauce separately.

MRS. SPENCER'S SWEDISH RECIPE

Baked Pike

The fish.   Cream or top of the milk.
Breadcrumbs.   Beaten egg.

Clean the fish, remove head and scales, and cut into pieces. Roll the pieces in beaten egg and dip in breadcrumbs. Place in a buttered fireproof dish and bake in the oven. Ten minutes before serving, pour over the cream and put back in the oven. The breadcrumbs will take up the cream, and the dish can then be placed under the grill for a minute or two to brown off the top.

MRS. SPENCER'S SWEDISH RECIPE

Ruffe

Cook as Pike.

[34]

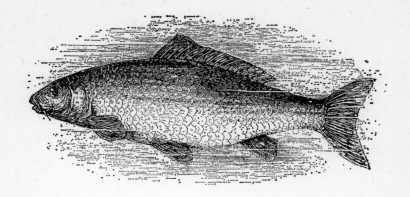

Carp

When preparing carp for cooking it is best to give them a good soak to remove the muddy flavour. Two soaks in salted water, followed by one soak in salted water with a little vinegar added. This is done after scaling and cleaning. Be very careful when removing the head to take away the gall stone which is just behind it, or the fish will taste bitter.

Delicious Carp

Put a handful of prepared, washed and chopped sorrel, a piece of butter, a piece of bread, chopped chives, parsley, and shallots into a saucepan, and simmer for 10 minutes; add some cream and simmer till mixed. Hardboil three eggs, chop the yolks and add to the mixture with three raw yolks, salt and black pepper. Stuff the cleaned carp with this mixture and sew it up, put the whole to marinate in oil seasoned with salt, pepper, chives, garlic, thyme, and bayleaf. When ready, grill, basting with the marinade.

Put chopped mushrooms in a saucepan and simmer in a little butter, let them cool and add a pinch of flour, capers, chopped anchovies, parsley, chives, shallots, butter, stock, salt and pepper. Cook gently and finish with a little lemon juice or a dash of vinegar.

Serve the carp on a hot dish with this sauce.

MANUEL DE LA FRIANDAISE, 1796

Carp à la Russe

The fish.	Glazed onions.
Flour.	Mushrooms.
Butter.	Sour cream.
2 glasses dry white wine.	1 tablespoonful vinegar.
Sauerkraut.	2 tablespoonfuls grated cheese.

Clean and scrape the fish and cut it into sections. Roll the pieces in seasoned flour and place in a buttered oven dish. Add the white wine and heat on a low flame until the wine is almost boiling, then put the pan in a moderate oven. Have ready some sauerkraut, and the glazed onions and mushrooms. When the fish is cooked, add some sour cream and the vinegar to the gravy, and the cheese. Serve the fish on a bed of the vegetables with the gravy over. Garnish with small pickles.

"GUIDE TO GOOD FOOD AND WINES" ANDRÉ SIMON *Collins*

Blue Carp

The fish.   Mixed herbs.
Sliced onions.   Peppercorns.
Wine vinegar.

Clean the fish but do not scale. Tie the fish head to tail in a circle and put into a pan, covered with vinegar. Bring to the boil and add other ingredients. Simmer very gently until the fish is tender, but still firm. Lift out carefully, and wash in hot water. Serve on a hot dish with whipped fresh cream, horseradish cream, or browned butter containing chopped capers and parsley.

"500 RECIPES FROM ABROAD" MARGUERITE PATTEN
Paul Hamlyn

Izaak Walton's Recipe for Cooking Carp

Take a Carp, alive if possible, scour him, and rub him clean with water and salt, but scale him not; then open him; and put him, with his blood and his liver, which you must save when you open him, into a small pot or kettle; then take sweet marjoram, thyme, and parsley, of each half a handful, a sprig of rosemary, and another of savoury; bind them into two or three small bundles and put them in your Carp, with four or five whole onions, twenty pickled oysters, and three anchovies. Then pour upon your Carp as much claret wine as will only cover him; and season your claret well with salt, cloves, and mace, and the rinds of oranges and lemons. That done, cover your pot and set it on a quick fire till it be sufficiently boiled. Then take out the Carp; and lay it with the broth, into the dish; and pour upon it a quarter of a pound of the best fresh butter, melted, and beaten with half a dozen spoonfuls of the broth, the yolks of two or three eggs, and some of the herbs shred. Garnish your dish with lemons, and so serve it up. And much good do you.

"THE COMPLEAT ANGLER"

[37]

Perch

"Perch and small boys have a good deal in common. Both species go around in gangs of anything from two to two dozen or more. Both species are rather greedy, rather ferocious and rather beautiful. In fact I would say that the perch is more beautiful than the boy, though not nearly so interesting."

"FISHING FOR BEGINNERS" MAURICE WIGGIN

Beignets de Perche de Tante Maria Duborgel

The fish.	White of egg.
Flour.	Brandy.
Olive oil.	Lemon quarters.
	Salt.

Take any sized perch, clean, skin, and fillet it. Make a batter as follows: Put into a bowl a quarter of a pound of water, add a pinch of salt and stir in just before the mixture is completely blended. Stirring all the time add a spoonful of olive oil and a spoonful of brandy. Leave the batter until just before you use it, then fold in a white of egg beaten stiff. Cover the fillets with this mixture, and put them into a very hot frying oil. Serve with lemon quarters.

"LA PÊCHE ET LES POISSONS DE RIVIÈRE" MICHEL DUBORGEL
Libraire Hachette

Perch in White Wine

White wine.	2 oz. flour.
Salt and pepper.	Chopped parsley.
Bouquet garni.	Sliced onion.
2 oz. butter.	The fish.

[38]

Put the cleaned fish in a fireproof dish, and cover, with the white wine. Add salt, pepper, sliced onion and bouquet garni. Cook for a quarter of an hour until the fish flakes easily in the fingers. Remove the skin, and place the perch on a serving dish. Make a roux with the butter and flour and blend in the liquor in which the fish has cooked. Add some chopped parsley which has been lightly fried in butter and pour the sauce over the fish. Serve very hot.

"LA PÊCHE ET LES POISSONS DE RIVIÈRE" MICHEL DUBORGEL
Libraire Hachette

Bleak, Loach, and Gudgeon

Three little fishes hardly worth cooking, but if you must, look up the recipes for smelt and cook them likewise.

Roach and Rudd

These two fish of the carp family make good eating just cleaned, dipped in milk, rolled in seasoned flour, and fried in butter. Serve with melted butter and slices of lemon.

Bream

Stuffed Bream

1 bream weighing 1½–2 lb.	Flour.
1 oz. butter.	1 tablespoonful lemon juice.
Salt and pepper.	Forcemeat.

For the Forcemeat

½ small onion, chopped.	1 dessertspoonful chopped
1 oz. butter.	parsley.
1 oz. grated cheese.	Grated lemon rind.
2 oz. sliced mushrooms.	Salt and pepper, nutmeg,
1 small cupful cooked rice.	Cayenne pepper.
1 tablespoonful chopped	4 tablespoonfuls cream.
chives.	1 beaten egg.

Fry the onion and mushroom in butter and mix with the rice and cheese, add all other ingredients and blend well.

Wash and clean the fish and put nearly all the butter in the bottom of a fireproof dish. Stuff the fish with the forcemeat and place in the dish. Sprinkle it with flour and seasoning, and dot with the rest of the butter, then sprinkle with the lemon juice. Cover the dish with greased paper or foil, and bake in a moderate oven for 40–50 minutes according to the size of the fish. This recipe can also be used for fresh haddock, hake, halibut, or cod.

Breme à la Mode du Pecheur

The fish.   White wine.

Shallots.   Butter.   Breadcrumbs.

Place the cleaned fish upon a bed of chopped shallots and breadcrumbs, in a fireproof dish, and cover the fish with the same mixture. Add the white wine and pats of butter and cook in a medium oven for 25 minutes, adding wine and butter as needed to keep the fish moist.

"GUIDE TO GOOD FOOD AND WINES" ANDRÉ SIMON *Collins*

Baked Bream

The fish.   Lemon.   2 large onions.

Breadcrumbs.   2 cloves garlic.   Oil.

Clean the fish and remove head and fins. Score the sides. Chop the onion and garlic and place this in the bottom of a fireproof dish. Slice the lemon thinly and put one slice in each of the scores of the fish. Lay the fish in the dish and squeeze the juice from any of the lemon that is left over on to the fish. Pour two tablespoonfuls of oil over the fish and sprinkle with breadcrumbs. Cover with lid or aluminium foil and cook in a moderate oven for 30 minutes. Remove the foil and leave the fish in the oven until the breadcrumbs are browned and the fish is cooked right through. Serve very hot.

MRS. PILCHER'S RECIPE

Tench

"The tench is the physician of fishes, for the Pike especially, and that the Pike, being either sick or hurt, is cured by the touch of the Tench. And it is observed that the tyrant Pike will not be a wolf to his physician, but forbears to devour him though he be never so hungry."

IZAAK WALTON

Tench à la Poulette

The fish.   ½ litre white wine.   2 oz. butter.
Salt and pepper.   1 oz. flour.   Bouquet garni.

Cook the cleaned fish in court bouillon, and remove the skin. Cut into small pieces. Make a roux with the butter and flour and add the wine, let this cook for 10 minutes, gently, stirring with a wooden spoon. Add the pieces of fish, the bouquet garni, and the seasoning, and let it simmer gently for 10 minutes more. Then blend into this two beaten egg yolks. Remove the bouquet garni. Garnish with chopped parsley and serve hot.

"LA PÊCHE ET LES POISSONS DE RIVIÈRE" MICHEL DUBORGEL
Libraire Hachette

Stuffed Tench

The fish.   Breadcrumbs.   Chopped mushrooms.
Chopped parsley.   Hardboiled egg.   White wine.

Split and clean the fish and stuff with a mixture of mushroom, egg, breadcrumbs, and parsley. Place in a fireproof dish and cook in oven for 30 minutes basting frequently with white wine.

"LA PÊCHE ET LES POISSONS DE RIVIÈRE" MICHEL DUBORGEL
Libraire Hachette

Barbel

Not much of a fish to eat as it is terribly bony; though the French think more of it than we do.

"But the Barbel affords an angler choice sport, being a lusty and a cunning fish; so lusty and cunning as to endanger the breaking of an angler's line, by running his head forcibly towards any covert, or hole, or bank, and then striking at the line, to break it off, with his tail; and also so cunning, to nibble and suck off your worm close to the hook, and yet avoid the letting the hook come into his mouth."

"THE COMPLEAT ANGLER" IZAAK WALTON

Boiled Barbel in Court Bouillon

Clean the fish and boil in court bouillon. Serve in a sauce made by reducing two cupfuls of the court bouillon, thickened with a nut of butter, some chopped parsley and capers. If served cold, provide Mayonnaise or Vinaigrette sauce (see Chapter 7).

"LA PÊCHE ET LES POISSONS DE RIVIÈRE" MICHEL DUBORGEL
Libraire Hachette

Stuffed Barbel

Clean and split the fish and stuff with chopped mushrooms and hardboiled egg. Cook in a fireproof dish and serve covered with white sauce.

"LA PÊCHE ET LES POISSONS DE RIVIÈRE" MICHEL DUBORGEL
Libraire Hachette

Bass

There are several kinds of bass, which is also known as "Sea-dace", "Sea Perch", or "Sea-wolf". They have a delicate taste and they can all be cooked according to any of the recipes for salmon, trout, or perch.

Stuffed Bass

The fish.   Seasoning.
Forcemeat.   White wine.
Streaky bacon.

Clean the fish. Make the forcemeat as in the recipe for stuffed bream. Fill the fish with the forcemeat and sew him up with needle and thread. Lay in a well buttered fireproof dish and put two or three strips of streaky bacon across him. Pour in a wineglassful of white wine, and bake in a moderate oven till the fish is done, adding more wine if necessary to keep moist, and basting frequently.

MRS. FINN *from the Tackle and Bait Shop at Deal*

Poached Bass

Put the fish into a salted court bouillon and bring it to the boil, then poach very gently till tender. Drain, and serve with Sauce Hollandaise.

CHAPTER THREE

EELS	CRAB
CONGER EEL	SCALLOPS
LAMPREYS	MUSSELS
COCKLES	OYSTERS
CRAWFISH	CRAYFISH
SHRIMPS	PRAWNS
LOBSTER	WINKLES

Eels

"And others say, that Eels, growing old, breed other Eels out
of the corruption of their own age; which, Sir Francis Bacon
says, exceeds not ten years. And others say, that as pearls are
made of glutinous dew drops, which are condensed by the suns
heat in those countries, so Eels are bred of a particular dew,
falling in the months of May or June on the banks of some
particular ponds or rivers, apted by nature of that end; which
in a few days are, by the sun's heat, turned into Eels: and
some of the Ancients have called the Eels that are thus bred,
the offspring of Jove."

"THE COMPLEAT ANGLER" IZAAK WALTON

Jellied Eels

2 lb. eels.	1 sprig of parsley.
1 large onion.	2 pints cold water.
1 bay leaf.	Whites and shells
1 tablespoonful vinegar.	of two eggs.
2 oz. leaf gelatine.	Salt and pepper.

Clean and skin the eels and put into a saucepan with the
water and all ingredients except the eggs and gelatine. Simmer
until the eels are tender. Take out the fish, cut into pieces
and remove the bones. Strain the liquid and return to the pan,
and add the crushed egg shells and lightly whisked whites of
the eggs. Add the gelatine and bring to the boil. Simmer for
2 minutes and strain again. Line a mould with the pieces of
eel, add the jelly and leave to set.

[46]

Eels Matelote

Eels.	Bouquet garni.
Red wine.	Garlic.
Salt and pepper.	Bread fried in
Onion.	butter.

Clean and skin the eels, cut them into pieces and stew gently in red wine and water seasoned with the other ingredients. At the same time brown some small onions in butter and then add this to the fish. Remove the bouquet garni and pour the fish and the sauce over thin slices of bread fried in butter.

Grilled Eel

Clean and skin the eels and cut them into chunks. Dip in flour, or breadcrumbs, and grill or fry. Serve with tomato sauce, or with lemon slices and chopped parsley.

Conger Eel

Conger Eel can be cooked in any way suitable for white fish.

Stewed Conger Eel

Onions.	Cider.
Butter.	Eel.
Flour.	

Brown two chopped onions in two ounces of butter, and then thicken with two tablespoonfuls of plain flour. Add the sliced eel, and season with salt and pepper. Add enough cider to cover the fish and then cover the dish with a lid or with foil, and place in the oven, cooking slowly for an hour. Serve the fish in the sauce, thickening it further with flour if necessary.

"GUIDE TO GOOD FOOD AND WINES" ANDRÉ SIMON *Collins*

Jersey Conger Soup

Conger eel.	6 borage leaves.
2 shallots.	12 marigold petals.
1 cabbage.	Salt and pepper.
1 pint fresh peas.	Parsley.
$\frac{1}{2}$ pint milk.	Thyme.
1 dessertspoonful flour.	Butter.
1 dessertspoonful vinegar.	Lemon.

Wash the fish and put in a saucepan with a quart of water, add the salt and pepper, parsley and thyme. Simmer for 30 or 40 minutes. Strain the liquid and put it in another saucepan.

Wash and shred the cabbage, chop the shallots and borage. Add these, with the peas, to the boiling liquid and cook till tender. Mix the flour with a little milk and thicken the soup with this and cook for 5 minutes. Add the rest of the milk and a small piece of fresh butter, and serve the soup with the marigold petals floating on it.

If preferred, the conger pieces can be eaten as a separate dish.

Sennen Cove Conger Stew

1 saucepan full of potatoes.	Court bouillon or water. Salt.
Milk.	Parsley.

Wash the conger and cut into finger-sized strips, heaps of them. Place on the potatoes and season well, add parsley, milk and court bouillon or water to cover. Put on the lid and simmer until done.

Lampreys

Henry the First, known as Henry Beauclerk, was never known to be guilty of any other excess in eating or drinking, but he died of "a surfeit of lampreys". One would like to know his recipe in order to avoid it! Possibly his cook did not remove the two filaments in the back of the creature, which are poisonous. If you still want to eat lampreys try them this way:

Lampreys Matelote

Put a pound of lampreys in half a litre of boiling red wine. Cook for one hour and thicken with melted butter and flour.

Stuffed Lamprey

1 medium sized lamprey.	1 egg.
Suet forcemeat (parsley and thyme stuffing).	Breadcrumbs.
	1 lemon.
Anchovy sauce.	

Rub the fish with salt, wash, and remove the poisonous cartilage and strings down the back. Fill the body with the stuffing and sew it up. Butter some greaseproof paper and wrap the fish up in it. Cover with hot water and simmer for 20 minutes. Drain and dry. Melt some butter in a baking dish and put in the fish. Bake for half an hour in a moderate oven, basting frequently. Strip off the skin, brush the fish with beaten egg and coat with breadcrumbs. Bake until browned and serve garnished with lemon, with anchovy sauce.

Crab

Crabmeat Casserole

1 cup of cooked crabmeat.	Pinch of cayenne.
3 cups of milk.	$\frac{1}{2}$ pound grated cheese.
Plain flour.	1 green pepper.
Butter.	4 oz. mushrooms.
Seasoning.	Breadcrumbs or flaky pastry.

Make a thick white sauce by heating 2 oz. of butter in a pan, adding two tablespoonfuls of flour, and the milk stirred in very gradually. Then add the cheese, stirring until smooth over a very low flame, or in a double boiler. Then add all the ingredients except the breadcrumbs (or pastry) and mix well.

Put the mixture in a shallow casserole or fireproof dish, cover with breadcrumbs (or pastry) and bake in a moderate oven till browned. If breadcrumbs are used for the cover, put on a few dabs of butter, and sprinkle with cayenne pepper. This dish can also be served baked in empty crab shells or individual dishes.

Boiled Crab. Dressed

Crab should be boiled by placing in cold water and bringing gradually to the boil. This method seems to inflict less pain than plunging them into boiling water. Cook for 20 minutes after it has come to the boil. Remove all the meat from the body and the claws, keeping the claw meat separate. Discard the entrails. Mix together the coral, or red meat, and the body meat and season with a few drops of oil, and lemon juice, or vinegar. Then shred the claw meat and season likewise. Arrange the meat back in the washed and dried crab shell with the body meat and coral across the middle and the claw meat each side.

Crab Newburg

$\frac{1}{2}$ lb. cooked crab meat.	Salt.
	Cayenne.
1 cup of cream.	2 egg yolks.
2 oz. butter.	Tablespoonful sherry.

Cook the crab meat in the butter for about 5 minutes, then add the seasonings and sherry. Blend the egg yolks and cream. Remove the crab from the stove and add the egg mixture then reheat in a double saucepan till the mixture thickens, being very careful that it does not boil. Serve on rounds of hot buttered toast, or on muffins.

Crawfish

This is a spiny lobster without claws which is caught around our southwestern coasts, is nearly as good as lobster to eat and is cooked the same way. Don't confuse it with 'crayfish' which is a little fresh water lobster.

Crawfish Curry

1 crawfish.	1 teaspoonful curry paste.
2 onions.	1 oz. flour.
1 apple.	2 oz. butter.
½ pint milk.	Salt.
1 tablespoonful coconut.	Boiled rice.
1 teaspoonful curry powder.	

Boil the crawfish and split him open, remove the uneatable parts and pick out all the meat from the body and the claws, and the creamy parts from the head. Cut the flesh up small. Peel and chop the onions and the apple, and cook in the melted butter for 15 minutes without browning. Add the curry powder and paste and a little milk. When this is thoroughly cooked add the crawfish. Soak the grated coconut in the rest of the milk for half an hour then strain the milk and use it to mix the flour to a smooth paste. Stir this into the curry, bring to the boil and add salt to taste. Simmer very gently for half an hour and serve with plain boiled rice and garnish with cut lemon and parsley.

[53]

Lobster

Boiled Lobster

Heat enough court bouillon to cover the lobster, and when this is boiling, holding the live lobster in the middle of the back, put it in head first. Cover, and cook for 20 minutes or a little more if it is a big lobster. Let him cool in the liquid.

Pull off the small claws and pick out the meat. Crack the big claws, removing meat if required or leaving it in if the lobster is to be served cold in his shell. Split the tail right down with a sharp knife, and the body, being careful not to break the stomach, a small sac just behind the head. Remove all traces of the intestinal canal which shows as a dark thread down the tail. Throw away the spongy tissue which lies between the meat and the shell. Remove the intestinal cord from the body also, and remove the stomach if the shell is to be used to hold the meat. Keep any bright red coral, and the green liver for sauce or garnish.

Lobster Thermidor

Boiled lobster.
2 tablespoons butter.
A little minced onion.
A pinch of cayenne
  pepper.
1 tablespoonful tomato
  puree.
Grated cheese.
$\frac{1}{2}$ glass dry white wine.
1 cup white sauce.
$\frac{1}{2}$ lb. mushrooms, chopped.

Take all the meat out of the lobster and cut small. Heat the butter and put the lobster into it with the onion, the pepper and the white wine. Cook gently for 5 minutes and then add the mushrooms and the tomato puree. Cook this mixture for a few minutes and then put it into the lobster shells, on a fireproof dish. Pour the white sauce over and sprinkle with grated cheese and bake briefly in a hot oven. Brown off under the grill and serve piping hot.

Mexican Lobster

Cooked lobster.
Oil.
1 large onion.
1 green pepper.
1 lb. cooked tomatoes.
Salt.
1 oz. sugar.
Pinch of ground
  cloves.
Bay leaf.
$\frac{1}{4}$ lb. mushrooms.
Tabasco sauce.

Cut the lobster into small pieces. Put three tablespoonfuls of oil into a pan and add the onion, tomatoes and pepper chopped small and all the seasonings, and simmer for 15 minutes. Take out the bay leaf and add the mushrooms and the lobster, and another two tablespoonfuls of oil. Simmer until all is heated through and serve.

C.A.I. ENCYCLOPAEDIA

Crayfish

A small freshwater lobster. In America there is another species of freshwater lobster they call a Crawfish!

> *"I went to the Bayou just last night*
> *There wasn't no moon but the stars were bright*
> *Got a big long hook on a big long pole*
> *And I pulled Mr. Crawfish out of his hole.*
> *See I got 'um, see the size*
> *Strooped and cleaned before your eyes*
> *Sleek in look. Fresh and ready to cook*
> *Now take Mr. Crawfish in your hand*
> *He's gonna look good in a frying pan.*
> *Fry him crisp or boil him right*
> *He'll be sweeter than sugar with every bite."*

Ecrevisses en Buisson

Just boil your crayfish in white wine court bouillon for about 10 minutes, drain, and serve cold. The central portion of the fan shaped tail should be removed, taking the black spinal cord with it.

Crayfish Risotto

Crayfish.	Butter.
Onion.	Flour.
$\frac{1}{4}$ lb. rice.	Cream.

Boil the crayfish in court bouillon as above. Melt some butter and cook the chopped onion in it until just coloured, then add the rice slowly. Then pour over this enough of the

[56]

court bouillon to cook the rice. Put all in a double boiler and cook slowly till the rice is done. Meanwhile shell the crayfish and drop them in melted butter and cook until coloured. Sprinkle with a little flour and add enough cream to cover the crayfish. Cook until just on the boil, stirring all the time. Serve the crayfish piled on the rice.

"GUIDE TO GOOD FOOD AND WINES" ANDRÉ SIMON *Collins*

Crayfish à la Meunière

Sauté the crayfish in very hot butter, and when well browned, season with salt and pepper, powdered thyme and bay leaf. Put in a fireproof dish and add enough dry white wine to cover the fish. Cover and bake in a hot oven for 20 minutes. Drain but retain the stock. Boil the stock down by half and thicken with a little blended flour and butter, pour over the crayfish and serve garnished with parsley.

Cockles

Cockle Soup

2 quarts fresh cockles.	Small stick of celery, chopped.
1½ oz. butter.	1 oz. flour.
2 pints cockle liquid.	Chopped parsley.
1 pint milk.	Pepper, salt.

Boil the cockles in plenty of water till they open. Strain the liquid, and shell the cockles. Heat the butter and blend in the flour. Gradually add the liquid and milk, stirring all the time. Add the chopped celery, salt, and pepper. Simmer for 30 minutes. Add the shelled cockles and the parsley and simmer for a few more minutes before serving.

Scallops

The shell of St. James, the emblem of the pilgrim.   Best eaten in January or February.

To Open Scallops

Place the shells on the stove top and they will open by themselves. Remove the beard, and black parts, but leave the coral.

Coquilles Saint Jacques à la Bretonne

4 scallops.	1½ oz. white breadcrumbs.
½ onion.	2 oz. butter.
1 shallot.	Salt and pepper.
Chopped parsley.	1 tablespoonful brandy.

1 gill dry white wine.

Chop the onion and shallot and cook in the butter until soft. Add the washed scallops, cut into quarters, and add the wine and brandy. Bring to simmering point and add breadcrumbs, parsley, pepper, and salt. Simmer for a few minutes and then put the mixture back into the scallop shells. Brown the breadcrumbs and sprinkle over the mixture in the shells. Dot with butter, and pipe a thin border of Duchess potatoes round the edge of each. Brown under the grill.

"THE IRIS SYRETT COOKERY BOOK" *Faber*

Baked Scallops

Breadcrumbs.	Salt and pepper.
Parsley.	Lemon juice.
Shallot.	Butter.

Take the scallops right out of the shells, and scrub the shells clean. Then line the shells with breadcrumbs, the chopped parsley and shallot and the seasoning. Put the scallops back in the shells and sprinkle more of the breadcrumb mixture on the top. Moisten the tops with melted butter and lemon juice and bake in a hot oven for about 20 minutes.

Mussels

Mussels should be washed well before cooking, and the shells scraped to remove any mud and beards. While they are being cooked the pan should be constantly shaken until the shells open, when the mussels are done.

Moules à la Mariniere

2 quarts mussels.
White wine court bouillon.
Butter.

Add the butter to the boiling court bouillon, add the cleaned mussels, cover with the lid, and shake over a hot flame for about 5 minutes, or until the shells open. Remove from the heat. Take one shell from each mussel, and pile the mussels in their half shells on to a dish, strain them over the liquor they were cooked in, and sprinkle with chopped parsley. Serve at once.

Mussel Pilaff

2 quarts mussels.	$\frac{1}{2}$ gill oil.
$\frac{1}{2}$ lb. rice.	Pinch of saffron.
1 chopped onion.	Stock.
2 oz. grated cheese	Bouquet garni.
(preferably Gruyere).	Seasoning.

Cook the cleaned mussels as above, and remove from their shells. Keep the liquor they were cooked in and strain it. Heat the oil and add the chopped onion, cooking until soft. Then add all the other ingredients. Total quantity of liquid should be three times the volume of the rice. Cover the dish and put it in a moderate oven for about 25 minutes. When cooked remove the bouquet garni, pile up the mixture on a dish and sprinkle with grated cheese.

"THE IRIS SYRETT COOKERY BOOK" *Faber*

Mussel Pudding

$\frac{1}{2}$ lb. S.R. flour.	Water.
3 oz. finely chopped suet.	Mussels.
Salt.	Pepper.

Make a suet crust, roll out and lay on a piece of greased greaseproof paper. Wash the mussels very well and remove the beards. Put them in a pan without liquid over a very low flame, and they will open almost immediately. Scoop them out on to the dough, turn in the edges to cover the mussels, wrap the paper round, enclose the whole in a pudding cloth and tie well and steam for $1\frac{1}{2}$ hours.

[62]

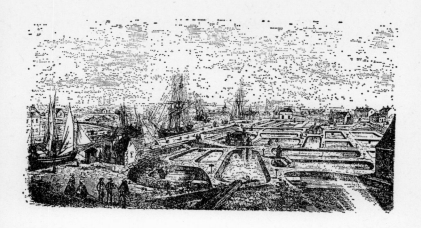

Oysters

"Honesty dwells like a miser in a poor house, As your pearls in your foul oyster."

SHAKESPEARE

The native, which is an oyster from Colchester or Whitstable, or other Kentish or Essex beds, should be eaten exactly as it is. Open the oyster by inserting the knife at the hinge and snapping the ligament which attaches the oyster to the flat shell. Serve in the other half of the shell in its own liquor.

Imported oysters may be cooked.

Angels on Horseback

Use large oysters and cook them in their own liquor by simmering until the edges curl. If they are cooked too long they will be very tough. Then drain the oysters and wrap each one in a piece of bacon, tying round with thread. Grill until the bacon is crisp and serve on toast.

[63]

Browned Oysters in Brown Sauce

Oysters.　　Lemon juice.
Flour.　　Worcestershire sauce.
Butter.　　Pepper and salt.

Open and drain the oysters, and dip each one in flour. Heat the butter and cook the oysters until brown. Make a roux with butter and flour and stir in the liquid from the cooked oysters. Season with salt, pepper, lemon juice and Worcestershire sauce to taste. Bring to the boil, and then pour over the oysters which have been put on toast. Serve with slices of lemon.

C.A.I. ENCYCLOPAEDIA

Fried Oysters

Just dip in egg and breadcrumbs and fry in hot fat.

Shrimps and Prawns

"Walking by the seaside, in a calm evening, upon a sandy shore, and with an ebbing tide, I have frequently remarked the appearance of a dark cloud, or rather very thick mist, hanging over the edge of the water, to the height, perhaps, of half a yard, and of the breadth of two or three yards, stretching along the coast as far as the eye could reach, and always retiring with the water. When this cloud came to be examined it proved to be nothing else than so much space filled with young shrimps, in the act of bounding into the air from the shallow margin of the water, or from the wet sand. If any motion of a mute animal could express delight, it was this; if they had meant to make signs of their happiness, they could not have done it more intelligibly. Suppose then, what I have no doubt of—each individual of this number to be in a state of positive enjoyment; what a sum, collectively, of gratification and pleasure we have here before our view."

"PALEY"

Shrimp de Jonghe

1 lb. of cleaned shrimps.   1 oz. butter.
2 tablespoonfuls of   1 clove of garlic, chopped.
  white wine.   2 tablespoonfuls chopped
Pepper, salt.   leek.
    2 slices of dried bread, crumbed.

Put the shrimps in a fireproof dish, add the wine and pepper, and dot with butter. Add the garlic, leek, and salt to the breadcrumbs and rub together until they are a smooth paste. Spread this over the shrimps, and bake in the oven (moderate) for 20 minutes.

Creamed Shrimps

Shrimps.   Celery salt.
White sauce.   Green pepper.

Make a smooth white sauce and flavour it with celery salt. Add the shrimps, and a tablespoonful of green pepper chopped very fine. Heat till boiling and serve on hot buttered toast.

Shrimp Rarebit

$\frac{1}{2}$ cup milk.   Pinch of cayenne pepper.
4 oz. cheese.   Salt.
Dessertspoonful $\frac{1}{2}$ pint cleaned shrimps.
  Worcestershire sauce. 1 egg.

Melt the grated cheese in the milk, and add the seasonings and Worcestershire sauce. Then add the shrimps and simmer gently till they are heated through. Remove from heat and add the beaten egg. Reheat till the mixture thickens but do not boil. Make pieces of toast and butter them, and then pour

[66]

the mixture over the toast, making sure that you cover every bit. Then put under the grill till the mixture begins to bubble and the top is browned.

JANE BEEDELL'S RECIPE

Scampi

Prawns.	Batter.
Sauce tartare.	Lemon.

Be sure that the prawns are dry. Dip them in batter and lower into hot deep fat and fry for 4 minutes only. Drain, and serve with slices of lemon and sauce tartare.

Prawns in Soya Sauce

8 oz. prawns.	2 tablespoonfuls sherry.
3 slices ginger.	1 dessertspoonful sugar.
3 tablespoons soya sauce.	1 dessertspoonful salt.
1 small onion (Spring onions when available).	1 dessertspoonful cornflour.

Wash the prawns and clip the whiskers and feet, but do not remove the shells. Make the sauce by blending the cornflour with a little water, adding the sherry, sugar, salt, and soya, and bring to the boil and thicken. Heat some frying oil and drop in the prawns, the sliced ginger and the sliced onion (about three tablespoonfuls of oil will be plenty). Then add the sauce and heat all together for about 10 minutes.

"500 RECIPES FROM ABROAD" MARGUERITE PATTEN

Prawn Patties

Puff pastry patty cases.
½ pt. thick white sauce.
1 oz. butter.
4 oz. prawns.
5 oz. cooked peas.
½ green pepper sliced.
1 blade of celery, chopped.
½ clove of garlic.
Paprika.
Salt and pepper.

Heat the butter and fry the prawns and the peas gently for two minutes, then add the celery and the pepper, sliced small. Cook for a minute or two then add the garlic, crushed. Make the thick white sauce and add the salt and pepper, stir well, then add all the other ingredients except paprika, which is used to garnish the finished article. Allow to cool, then fill the pastry cases with the mixture, put a whole prawn on top of each and sprinkle with paprika.

Curried Prawns

1 small onion.
2 oz. butter.
2 oz. flour.
Teaspoonful curry powder.
Salt and pepper.
Cupful of thick cream.
1 oz. sultanas.
1 pt. prawns.

Sauté the sliced onion in butter, then add the flour and curry powder, blending well, add salt and pepper and cream. Heat the sultanas and prawns in this sauce, and serve with boiled rice.

CHAPTER FOUR

FLOUNDER
DAB
PLAICE
SOLE
HALIBUT
TURBOT
SKATE
BRILL

"Remember that the Wit and Invention of Mankind were bestowed for other Purposes than to deceive silly Fish: and that however delightful Angling may be, it ceases to be innocent when used otherwise than as a mere recreation."

RICHARD BROOKS ON ANGLING, 1766

THE SEA FISHER

"First of all the fisher should have body and limbs both swift and strong, neither over fat nor lacking in flesh. For often he must fight with mighty fish in landing them, which have exceeding strength so long as they circle and wheel in the arms of their mother the sea.

"Cunning of wit too, and wise should the fisher be, since many and various are the devices that fishes contrive, when they chance upon unthought-of snares. Daring also should he be and dauntless and temperate, and he must not love satiety of sleep, but must be keen of sight, wakeful of heart, and open eyed. He must bear well the wintry weather and the thirsty season of Sirius: he must be fond of labour, and he must love the sea. So shall he be successful in his fishing and dear to Hermes."

OPPIAN "HALIEUTICA"

Flounder

Swedish Rolled Fillets with Lemon Sauce

This dish can be made with any flat fish, but is especially good made with flounder.

Filleted flounder. Court bouillon.
Shrimps.   Lemon slices.
    Dill or parsley.
    Lemon Sauce.

Make each fillet into a roll and skewer with a cocktail stick. Place in a saucepan and cover with court bouillon. Simmer for 10 minutes. Drain the fish and keep hot on a plate while making the sauce. Pour the sauce over the unskewered fillets garnish with the shrimps, parsley or dill, and the lemon sections.

"500 FOREIGN DISHES" MARGUERITE PATTEN

Lemon Sauce (see Chapter 7).

Fried Fillets of Flounder

Dip the fillets in beaten egg, and then in breadcrumbs, and fry in butter. Or dip in flour and fry in deep fat.

Dab

Cook in the same way as flounder.

Dab and Roe Stuffing

6 dabs.	Lemon juice.
Roe stuffing.	1 oz. butter.

Cut off the heads of the fish and wash. Remove the dark skin. Cut the fish down that side as if for filleting and lift the flesh but do not remove. Fill with the roe stuffing. Place the fish in a fireproof dish and sprinkle with lemon juice. Pour melted butter over the fish and bake for 20 minutes in a moderate oven. Serve with Hollandaise Sauce (see Chapter 7).

Roe Stuffing

4 soft herring roes.	$\frac{1}{2}$ oz. flour.
Milk.	Pinch cayenne.
Salt and pepper.	Lemon juice.
$\frac{1}{2}$ oz. flour.	Tablespoonful breadcrumbs.

Wash the roes and place them in a fireproof dish and just cover with milk. Add seasoning, cover with a lid or foil, and cook in a very slow oven for 30 minutes. Melt the butter in a saucepan and mix in the flour. Add the milk from the roes and cook till the sauce thickens. Add the beaten roes to the cooled sauce. Season to taste, and add breadcrumbs if the mixture is not thick enough.

[72]

Plaice

Plaice is in season from May until Christmas, and is best eaten filleted and fried.

Fried Plaice

Either dip the filleted plaice in seasoned flour and fry in a shallow pan, or dip into seasoned flour, and coat with egg and breadcrumbs, or dip into batter, and fry in deep fat.

Serve with Sauce Tartare (see Chapter 7).

Stuffed Plaice

1 large plaice about 1½ lb.	Browned breadcrumbs.
½ pint seasoned brown stock.	Stuffing.

Remove the dark skin only from the plaice and cut down the centre as for filleting, on that side only. Raise the fillets but do not remove them. Fill the cavity with the stuffing and place in a fireproof dish. Pour the stock over and bake for 45 minutes in a moderate oven. Sprinkle over the browned breadcrumbs just before serving.

Stuffing

4 tablespoonfuls breadcrumbs.	¼ teaspoonful dried herbs.
1 oz. chopped suet, or butter.	Grated lemon rind.
1 teaspoonful chopped parsley.	½ teaspoonful salt.
	½ teaspoonful pepper.
	Egg to bind.

Mix all the ingredients together.

Sole

Sole can be cooked in so many ways with so many sauces and vegetables. Dover sole is the best, and is quite different from Lemon sole, though both may be cooked in the same way.

Fillets de Sole Bonne Femme

8 fillets sole.

½ pint dry white wine.

1 sliced carrot.

1 sliced onion.

4 oz. button mushrooms.

1½ oz. butter.

Juice of half a lemon.

2 tablespoons chopped parsley.

Salt and pepper.

Bouquet garni.

Sauce Hollandaise made
   with four yolks.

Wash and dry the fillets. Fold the ends under and place in a lightly buttered fireproof dish. Lay the sliced vegetables round, season well, and add the bouquet garni. Pour the wine over and cover the dish with buttered greaseproof paper, and then poach the fish in a moderate oven. Meanwhile, wipe and slice the mushrooms and place them in a pan with the butter, lemon juice, and seasoning. Cover with greaseproof paper and then the lid. Shake over a gentle heat for 5–7 minutes. Keep hot.

Make the Sauce Hollandaise (see Chapter 7) using 2 tablespoons of the fish liquor for the base. Add the mushrooms and parsley.

When the fish is cooked, remove it from the pan and place on a hot dish. Reduce the remaining liquor until only two tablespoonfuls remain, and add this to the sauce. Pour the sauce over the fish and place the dish under a very hot grill until the food is lightly browned.

"THE IRIS SYRETT COOKERY BOOK" *Faber*

Fillets of Sole Florentine

Fillets of sole.	Lemon juice.
Butter.	Leaf spinach.
Pepper and salt.	White sauce.

Cook the fillets of sole in butter, season with pepper and salt and lemon juice. Line a fireproof dish with leaf spinach boiled and drained and tossed in butter. Place the fillets of sole on the spinach, cover with white sauce, and brown in the oven.

"GUIDE TO GOOD FOOD AND WINES" ANDRÉ SIMON *Collins*

Fried Sole

Remove the dark skin and dip in flour, sprinkle with salt and pepper and lemon juice, and then dip into beaten egg and breadcrumbs and fry in pure oil, very hot.

Sole Duglere

1 sole.	Breadcrumbs.
2 tomatoes.	1 dessertspoonful
1 small onion.	tomato puree.
1 glass dry white wine.	1 oz. butter.
Parsley.	1 dessertspoonful flour.

Peel the tomatoes and remove the pips, and then chop them. Peel and chop the onion. Melt 1 oz. of butter and blend with the flour. Put the chopped vegetables and the parsley in a fireproof dish and lay the seasoned sole on them. Add the white wine, and cook gently in the oven. Remove the sole from the liquor and boil the liquor until it is reduced by half. Blend the flour and butter previously combined, with this liquor, add the tomato puree. Pour the sauce over the sole and cook 5 minutes more in a hot oven.

[75]

Halibut

The best halibut is the smallest one, and if caught between March and October, it is specially good. Bigger halibut is usually cooked in steaks.

Chicken Halibut with Cheese Sauce

Fillet a small halibut and season with salt and lemon juice. Roll the fillets and place in a fireproof dish with a dab of butter on each. Cover the dish with foil and cook in a moderate oven until the fish is done. Serve with Cheese Sauce (see Chapter 7).

Baked Halibut

Halibut steaks can be cooked in much the same way as the fillets in the last recipe. Remove the dark skin by dipping the fish into boiling water before cooking, and season the fish well before putting it in a fireproof dish. Put some milk in the bottom of the dish to keep the fish moist and cook very gently. Serve the fish with any sauce suitable for white fish.

Turbot

The best of the large flat fish, turbot can be cooked "Bonne Femme" or "Florentine" as in the recipes for Sole, or in any of the ways suitable for white fish with any of the sauces.

Baked Turbot with Shrimp Sauce

> Turbot.
> Salt and pepper.
> Squeeze of lemon.
> Cream.

Slice the turbot into large pieces and place in a fireproof dish. Season with salt and pepper and a squeeze of lemon, and cover with cream. About half a pint should be plenty. Stand the dish in another dish of water, and bake slowly, basting frequently. When cooked, drain and place on a serving dish, and keep hot while you make the shrimp sauce (see Chapter 7).

Brill

Rather like Turbot but not quite so good, it should be cooked in the same way as Turbot or Sole.

Baked Brill with Crayfish

1 brill.	2 oz. butter.
2 tablespoonfuls finely chopped shallot.	1 teaspoonful finely minced herbs.
¼ lb. mushrooms.	Breadcrumbs.
1 gill stock.	6 crayfish cooked in
1 gill Madeira.	court bouillon (see page 15).

Clean the fish and score it across the back. Spread the minced shallot and mushrooms in a buttered baking dish and pour in the stock, and Madeira. Lay the fish in back down. Melt an ounce of butter in a saucepan and stir in as many white breadcrumbs as will absorb it. Add pepper, salt, and the herbs and spread over the fish. Bake for half an hour, basting frequently. When cooked, lift the fish carefully on to a flat dish and pour the gravy round, serve garnished with the crayfish, some fresh parsley, and sliced cucumber.

Skate

Skate au Gratin

Skate wings.   A little flour.
Sliced onions.   Butter.
Chopped shallot and parsley.   Breadcrumbs.
1 oz. sliced mushrooms.   Salt and pepper.

Skin the fish and cut into pieces. Put all ingredients into a buttered dish, except for the flour and butter. Cover with a lid and cook for about an hour at 350 deg. When cooked strain off the liquor, and make a roux with the flour and butter, adding this liquor. Pour the sauce over the fish and sprinkle with breadcrumbs. Brown under the grill.

Skate with Black Butter

2 lb. skate wings.   1 tablespoonful
4 oz. butter.   chopped parsley.
Court bouillon.   2 tablespoonfuls
2 tablespoonfuls capers.   wine vinegar.

Wash the skate, and cut it into slanting pieces. Place the fish in the hot court bouillon and simmer for 20 minutes. Remove the fish and scrape off the skin. The fish is then placed on a serving dish and kept hot. The butter is melted in a sauté pan and when it is deep brown is poured over the fish. Heat the vinegar and reduce by half, pour this over the skate, and then sprinkle on the capers and chopped parsley.

[79]

I have waited with a long rod
And suddenly pulled a gold-and-greenish, lucent fish from below
And had him fly like a halo round my head,
Lunging in the air on the line.

Unhooked his gorping, water horny mouth,
And seen his horror tilted eye,
His red-gold, water-precious, mirror-flat bright eye:
And felt him beat in my hand, with his mucous, leaping life throb.

LINES FROM "FISH" D. H. LAWRENCE

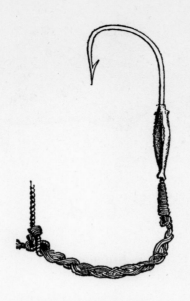

CHAPTER FIVE

COD	SHAD
HAKE	MULLET
HADDOCK	JOHN DORY
WHITING	WHITEBAIT
LING	SPRATS
POUTING	SMELT
HERRING	GURNARD
MACKEREL	DOGFISH
PILCHARD	

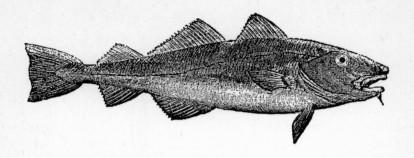

Cod

Swedish Boiled Cod

1 cod.	Butter.
Water.	Hardboiled eggs.
	Coarse salt.

Clean the fish and remove head, but keep in one piece. With a sharp knife score the sides of the fish deeply. Have your fish kettle ready with enough boiling water to cover, and put in a small handful of coarse salt. Place the fish in the water, and boil gently for about 8 minutes. Remove carefully and serve with plenty of melted butter into which you have chopped the hardboiled eggs.

MRS. SPENCER'S SWEDISH RECIPE

Fish Curry

1 lb. cod.	1 tablespoonful chopped parsley
1 oz. butter.	for garnish.
1 onion.	1 dessertspoonful Vencatachellums
2 tomatoes.	curry powder.
	2 teaspoonfuls lemon juice.

Chop the onion and fry lightly in the butter, then add all the other ingredients including the fish chopped into pieces. Add a little water and simmer for 20 minutes. Serve with boiled rice and garnish with chopped parsley.

Serve with popadums, sliced banana sprinkled with coconut, tomatoes chopped small and sprinkled with chopped chives moistened with vinegar. Many small savoury dishes go well with curry.

Danish Baked Cod with Mushroom Sauce

Cod cutlets.	Paprika.
Bacon.	Butter.
Salt.	

Cut up enough bacon into small pieces to cover the bottom of the fireproof dish you are going to use. Then rub the cod cutlets with salt and paprika and place them in the dish. Cut up some more bacon and put on top and dab with butter. Bake in a moderate oven for 40 minutes. Baste while cooking, and when done, strain off the liquid to add to the sauce. Make the sauce by cooking $\frac{1}{4}$ lb. mushrooms in a little milk, mix with the stock and thicken with cream.

Cod with Sweet and Sour Sauce

1 codling.	1 turnip.
1 oz. cornflour.	Oil.
1 onion.	Sweet and sour sauce
1 carrot.	(see Chapter 7).

Leave the head and tail on the cleaned fish, and score the sides of the fish about 1 inch apart. Make a paste of the cornflour with a little water and coat the fish with this. Cook the fish slowly in hot fat until just tender. Chop the vegetables and fry in the oil for 1 minute, add them to the sweet and sour sauce and pour over the fish.

[83]

Ling

Ling may be cooked by any recipe used for Cod. It fries well in slices.

Fried Sliced Ling

2 lb. ling.	Frying oil.
1 egg.	Flour.
Breadcrumbs.	Salt and pepper.

Wash and dry the fish and cut it into slices, sprinkle with salt and pepper then roll in flour. Brush with beaten egg and dip in breadcrumbs. Fry in hot oil, drain and serve with Sauce Tartare, or any white fish sauce.

Hake

A fish very like cod, with bones that are easy to remove. Cook hake by any recipe suitable for white fish. Recipes for fresh haddock and for cod are specially suitable for hake, but baking is probably the best way to cook this fish.

Haddock

If there is any sea fish more than another that requires good cooking, it is the one which, according to the legend, St. Peter drew out from the lake of Genesareth to obtain the tribute money, leaving the mark of his finger and thumb on its shoulders.

In season from September to February, fresh haddock may be cooked according to any recipe for white fish.

French Baked Haddock 'Aux Fines Herbes'

Haddock.	Parsley.
Mushrooms.	Garlic if liked.
Onions.	2 wineglassfuls white wine.

Place the haddock, which has been cleaned, and the head and fins removed, in a fireproof dish. Surround the fish with the chopped mushrooms, onions, and parsley, and the crushed clove of garlic if you like it. Pour the wine over the fish and bake in a moderate oven till done, basting frequently. Serve in the baking dish.

Grilled Fresh Haddock with Mustard Sauce

Haddock.
Butter.
Pepper and salt.

Take a small haddock and slit it down the back by the side of the bone. Clean it and remove the bone by slipping the point of a knife underneath and gently working away the flesh. Cut off the head, tail, and fins. Season the haddock inside, brush fish and grill with melted butter, and grill the fish on both sides till done. Serve with mustard sauce, and garnish with parsley. Mustard sauce (see Chapter 7).

Whiting

Whiting is tasteless but digestible, and can therefore be much improved by good cooking.

Fried Whiting

Split the fish and clean it, and remove the backbone. Sprinkle with salt and pepper and flour. Then dip in beaten egg and breadcrumbs. Melt sufficient butter in a pan and fry the fish in this. Serve with Maître d'Hôtel butter (see Chapter 7).

Or: Split the fish as above, and cut into fillets. Dip in batter and fry in oil. Serve with Sauce Tartare (see Chapter 7).

Merlans Bercy

4 large fillets or 4 whiting.	Butter.
3 shallots.	2 oz. mushrooms.
Wineglassful of white wine.	Lemon juice.
Salt and pepper.	Chopped parsley.

Place the whiting fillets, or the split and opened whole fish, in a buttered fireproof dish. Chop the shallots and put round the fish. Sauté the chopped mushrooms in butter. Season the fish and add the mushrooms, keeping back the butter they were cooked in. Pour the wine over the fish, and add the juice of a lemon.

Cook in a moderate oven, basting frequently. When cooked, put the fish in another hot dish, and reduce the liquid in which the fish cooked by half, then pour it over the fish. Sprinkle over the butter from the mushrooms, and grill till brown. Sprinkle with chopped parsley and serve.

Pouting

This is the fish you catch so easily when you are after something much better. Unfortunately, it doesn't keep for more than a few hours, and doesn't cook or eat well. So don't bother to cook it, not even for the cat.

The Angler's Tackling

My rod and my line, my float and my lead,
  My hook and my plummet, my whetstone and knife,
My basket, my baits, both living and dead
  My net, and my meat, for that is the chief;
Then I must have thread, and hairs green and small,
  With mine angling purse; and so you have all.

IZAAK WALTON "THE COMPLEAT ANGLER"

Herrings

A fish which is equal to any in flavour and nutritional value.

Grilled Herrings

Clean the fish and scale it, and remove the head. Wipe, and season with salt and pepper after scoring the sides deeply. Rub just a little olive oil over the fish and cook under a hot grill turning once. Serve with mustard sauce (see Chapter 7).

Harengs aux Betteraves

4 herring.	2 oz. butter.
1 large beetroot.	1 tablespoonful French mustard.
2 tablespoonfuls oil.	Seasoning.

Clean the fish, and place them in the oil in a shallow dish. Season well and allow to stand for an hour, turning from time to time. Then drain, and cook under a hot grill for about 3 minutes each side. Meanwhile, dice the beetroot. Melt half the butter in a pan, add the beetroot and heat it gently in the butter. Season. Melt the rest of the butter in a clean pan and stir in the mustard. Season well. Put the herrings in a long flat dish and put the beetroot garnish round the sides, pour the sauce over the herrings.

"THE IRIS SYRETT COOKERY BOOK" *Faber*

Potted Herrings

"Get herrings enough to fill up your dish
And into the stomach of each little fish
a peppercorn put; this will give it a flavour;
Then layers of alternate onion thin sliced.
And herrings and bay leaves—each layer well spiced
Then over the whole some vinegar pour;
Diluted with water—a pint or still more;
Three hours in the oven, with moderate heat,
Will make it quite fit for the hungry to eat."

Herrings Fried in Oatmeal

Clean a fresh herring, cut off its head, open it out flat by splitting it up the back. Take out the backbone and as many other bones as will come with it. Dip the fish in fine oatmeal and fry in shallow fat for 3 minutes on each side.

Soused Fillets of Herring

6 fresh herrings.	Pepper.
2 teaspoonfuls chopped chives.	Salt.
2 teaspoonfuls chopped parsley.	Boiling water.
2 bayleaves.	Vinegar.
12 peppercorns.	Salad oil.
Allspice.	Watercress.

Fillet the fish, then wash and dry, and lay on a board with the skin side down. Sprinkle with the chives, parsley, pepper, and salt. Roll up the fillets and bind firmly with tape. Put in a fireproof dish and sprinkle the spices, bayleaves, and salt on the top. Fill the dish with vinegar and water in the proportions of three parts of vinegar to one of water, and cover. Bake slowly in a moderate oven for 1 hour. Allow to cool and

[89]

then remove fish, wiping off any solids. Arrange on a dish and garnish with watercress. Season lightly with vinegar, salad oil, pepper, and salt.

Pilchard

Unfortunately pilchard do not travel well out of tins, so the only chance you will have to eat them fresh is if you catch them around our southwestern coasts. The Pilchard may be distinguished from the Herring by the fin, which is exactly in the middle of the back, while in the herring it is nearer to the tail.

They can be cooked in the same way as herrings.

Pilchard Hot Pot

Clean and scale the fish, split open and remove bones. Grease a fireproof dish and lay the fish in. Make a sauce with butter, flour, and milk, salt and pepper, tomato puree, to taste, and cover the fish with this. Partly boil some potatoes, slice and completely cover the fish with these. Dot with butter, grate a little cheese over, and bake for 15 minutes in a moderate oven. Brown under the grill and serve.

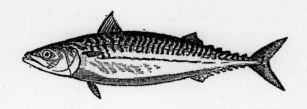

Mackerel

Some say that mackerel, fresh out of the sea and grilled, is the finest eating fish there is, and in the summer those who are lucky enough to be there when the mackerel are about go out with feathers or spinners and catch them, sometimes, as fast as they can be pulled in. It is only right that so handsome a fish should taste so fine, without complicated cooking or sauces. But mackerel spoils very quickly and must be cooked fresh. Never cook a mackerel that has gone limp and lost his glitter, he might be poisonous.

Grilled Mackerel

Clean the fish and cut off head and fins. Score deeply down each side several times. Grease the grill and place the fish on it, cooking until brown before turning over to do the other side.

Or, after cleaning split the fish and grill, cooking the open side first.

Season the fish with a pinch of salt and cayenne, and serve with Maître d'Hôtel butter (see Chapter 7), garnish with lemon slices and parsley.

Or, grill as in the first method, and when cooked open the fish and remove the backbone, and sprinkle with chopped shallot, tarragon and parsley, a pinch of salt and cayenne, and little dabs of butter. Put in a fireproof dish with just a little water and a splash of wine or vinegar, and cook in a hot oven for 5 minutes.

Soused Mackerel

Remove the heads and clean the fish, split and remove backbone. Roll from tail upwards and put in a fireproof dish. Cover with a half and half mixture of vinegar and water and add one peppercorn per fish. Cook for at least 2 hours in a slow oven. If liked, a bay leaf or a pinch of allspice can be added. Eat hot or cold.

Dry Fried Mackerel

Remove the head and clean the fish. Score deeply down each side and fry over a moderate heat in a dry pan. Serve in the same way as grilled mackerel.

Mackerel Balls

3 mackerel.	1 egg.
Teacupful of breadcrumbs.	Salt and pepper.

Clean and skin the fish, remove the bones. Put the fish through a mincer. Mix all the ingredients together and make into balls with the hands, not too big. Fry in hot fat. If the mixture is too moist, add more breadcrumbs.

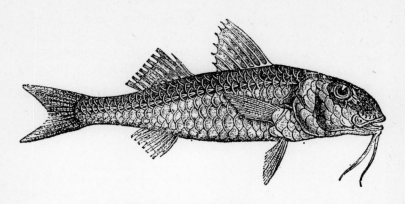

Red Mullet

"*The Mullet, when encircling seines inclose,*
The fatal threads and treacherous bosoms knows.
Instant he rallies all his vigorous powers
And faithful aid of every nerve implores:
O'er battlements of cork up-darting flies,
And finds from air the escape that sea denies.
But should the first attempt his hope deceive
And fatal space the imprisoned fall receive,
Exhausted strength no second leap supplies—
Self doomed to death, the prostrate victim lies;
Resigned, with painful expectation waits,
Till thinner elements complete his fates."

OPPIAN

"Mullets were often brought alive in glass vases to table, and a barbarous pleasure was derived from witnessing the changes of colour they underwent in expiring. Apicus invented a mode of suffocating the Mullet in a kind of pickle, and Seneca endeavoured to put an end to these practices, disgraceful to a people who stood foremost in ancient civilisation."

[93]

To Clean Mullet

Mullet, like woodcock, is usually eaten uncleaned, but if you don't like this clean in the usual way but leave the liver behind.

Rouget à la Nicoise

4 mullets.	6 green olives.
½ lb. ripe tomatoes.	Seasoned flour.
1 clove garlic.	Oil for frying.
8 anchovy fillets.	Seasoning with
6 black olives.	a pinch of sugar.

Scale and clean the fish if desired, and wash and dry well. Roll the fish in the seasoned flour and fry well on both sides in the hot oil, for about 6 minutes. Skin the tomatoes and cut them into quarters, sauté in another pan, in hot oil and garlic crushed with a little salt, the anchovy fillet, and the stoned olives. Season with pepper and mix gently. Spread this mixture over the fish; garnish with chopped parsley and slices of lemon.

"THE IRIS SYRETT COOKERY BOOK" *Faber*

Rougets au Safran

4 mullets.	2 oz. butter.
1 each onion, tomato, shallot.	3 egg yolks.
Pinch of saffron.	2 tablespoons thick cream.
1½ gills dry white wine.	1 oz. butter.
Seasoned flour.	Seasoning.

Wash and scale the fish, clean if desired. Score on the sides. Spread the butter in a fireproof dish and sprinkle with chopped shallot and onion. Roll the flesh in the seasoned flour and place in the dish. Mix the saffron with wine and water enough to cover the fish and pour it over. Dice the tomato and put on the fish and leave the whole to marinate for at least half an hour. Cover with greaseproof paper and cook gently, for a quarter of an hour. When cooked, drain the fish and lay on a serving dish. Whisk the egg yolks and cream and add to the liquor in a fresh pan, thicken over a low heat without boiling. Whisk in the remaining $\frac{1}{2}$ oz. butter. Season if needed and sprinkle with parsley. This is very good served with plain boiled rice.

"THE IRIS SYRETT COOKERY BOOK" Faber

Baked Mullet in Paper Cases

3 red mullet. $\frac{1}{2}$ oz. flour.   1 teaspoonful lemon juice.
Salad oil. $\frac{1}{2}$ oz. butter.
2 tablespoonfuls sherry.   Salt.
1 teaspoonful anchovy sauce.   Cayenne.

Sprinkle each mullet with a little salt. Cut three pieces of greaseproof paper large enough to roll the fish in and oil the paper well. Roll each fish up in a piece of the paper, tie the ends firmly and twist the string round once or twice to keep the paper together. Lay in a baking tin and cook in a moderate oven, for 20 minutes or a little more if the fish are big. Keep the fish hot. Melt the butter in a pan and add the flour, the liquor from the fish, the anchovy sauce, the lemon juice the pepper, and the sherry, in that order. Remove the string from the fish, but let them remain in the papers, lay on a hot dish, and serve with the sauce separately.

Dried Mullet Roe

Take out the roe whole and cover it with salt. Leave for 5 hours, then press, but not strongly, between two boards. Then wash, and dry in the sun, when it soon becomes fit for use.

OLD ITALIAN RECIPE

John Dory

Caught mostly in the Autumn and Winter John Dory is neglected by cooks in this country, but it is well worth cooking.

Dory Fillets Fried in Batter

Clean and bone the fish, cut into pieces; coat the fish with batter and fry till crisp. Serve with Sauce Tartare (see Chapter 7).

Boiled Dory

Clean the fish and remove head and fins. Place in a fish kettle and cover with equal parts of wine and water. Simmer till cooked. Remove the fish and strain; allow to cool and serve with a sauce of lemon juice and oil, and a sprinkling of salt and pepper. Or serve with Shrimp Sauce (see Chapter 7).

Whitebait

"The delicacy of Whitebait needs no comment. Pennant states it to be delicious, and says that epicures of the lower order resort to the taverns adjacent to the places where it is taken, for the purpose of enjoying it."

Fried Whitebait

Wash the fish well and dredge with flour. Shake in a sieve to separate each fish and to remove loose flour. Fry in deep fat for a few minutes, shaking gently to keep separated. Drain well on soft paper and serve with slices of lemon and brown bread and butter.

Don't put too many fish in the fat at once. Just a handful at a time. When all the fish are cooked, put the lot back in deep fry until they are crisp, before serving.

Devilled Whitebait

Cook as above, but divide into two piles, and sprinkle one pile with salt and cayenne pepper.

Sprats

In season from October to March.

Savoury Sprats

Sprats.	Parsley.
Dill.	Seasoning.

Bone the sprats; with the fingers break off the head and ease out the backbone with the thumb, bringing the gut with it, and opening the fish. Wash and drain well. Chop the dill and parsley very small and sprinkle it with salt and pepper. Press the inside of each fish into this so that it is coated with the mixture. Then press two fish face to face with the seasoning inside, and fry in a shallow pan in hot oil.

MRS. SPENCER'S SWEDISH RECIPE

Baked Sprats and Anchovy

Sprats.	Butter.
Tin of anchovies.	Breadcrumbs.
Seasoning.	

Bone the sprats as above and then roll each fish with a piece of anchovy in the middle. Pack the rolled fish in a fireproof dish, sprinkle with breadcrumbs and seasoning, and a few dabs of butter, and cook in a moderate oven.

MRS. SPENCER'S SWEDISH RECIPE

Sprats Fried in Batter

1 oz. butter.   Egg white.
Cold water.   Boiling water. $\frac{1}{4}$ lb. flour.   Parsley.   Lemon.

Make a batter by melting 1 oz. of butter in a tablespoonful of boiling water; add this to $\frac{1}{4}$ pint of cold water and stir it into a $\frac{1}{4}$ lb. of flour. Beat the white of an egg until it is stiff and blend it with the flour and water. Dip each washed and dried sprat into this and drop into deep fat. Serve very hot with fried parsley and lemon quarters, and brown bread and butter.

Broiled Sprats

Fasten fresh sprats in rows with a skewer run through the eyes, dredge with flour. Rub your grill with butter, and lay the sprats on, cook quickly till brown, turn over and cook the other side, and serve very hot with slices of lemon and brown bread and butter.

Smelt

The true smelt is in season from September to April, and smells of cucumber. The sand smelt is not so good a fish, but also smells faintly of cucumber and can be cooked in the same way as smelt.

Stewed Smelts

Put your smelts into a deep dish with white wine and water, a little rosemary and thyme, a piece of fresh butter and some large mace, and salt, let them stew half an hour, then take a handful of parsley and boil it, then beat it with the back of a knife, then take the yolks of three or four eggs, and beat them with some of your fish broth, then serve up your fish upon sippets, pour on your sauce, scrape on sugar, and serve it.

A TRUE GENTLEWOMAN'S DELIGHT. ELIZABETH GREY, 1682

Smelt à la Stoeher

1 lb. smelt.	$\frac{1}{2}$ cup fish bouillon.
A little water.	1 beaten egg yolk.
2 tablespoonfuls butter.	Grated cheese.
Pinch of salt.	Dessertspoonful flour.

Clean the fish and simmer until tender in water, with the salt and half the butter. Melt the remaining butter and blend in flour. Combine the court bouillon and egg yolk and add to the flour mixture and cook until it begins to thicken. Pour the sauce over the fish and grate cheese on top. Brown off under the grill.

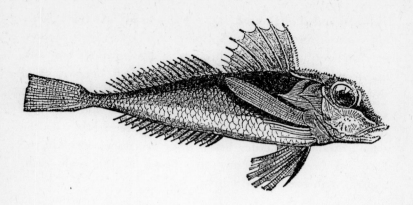

Red Gurnard

In season from July to April, this ugly little fish makes a noise like a cuckoo. Or possibly it is the cuckoo which makes a noise like a gurnard?

Broiled Gurnard

The fish must be cleaned and scraped, heads and fins removed, and then dried well. Score the sides of the fish deeply and then dip in flour, and brush over with melted dripping. Grease the grill with dripping, and cook slowly turning several times. Serve the fish hot with a sauce of melted butter.

Baked Gurnard

2 gurnards.	Lemon juice.
1 oz. butter.	3 tablespoonfuls
2 tablespoonfuls chopped	white wine.
mushrooms.	Pepper and salt.

2 tablespoonfuls browned breadcrumbs.

Clean and skin the fish and remove heads and fins. Score three times on each side. Sprinkle them with two teaspoonfuls of finely chopped mushrooms, a little pepper and salt, and lemon juice. Lay them in a well buttered, deep fireproof dish. Pour the wine over the fish, and put the butter, in dabs, on the top. Lay a thickly buttered paper over and bake in a quick oven until they are cooked, basting frequently with the wine. About 5 minutes before they are done, sprinkle the browned breadcrumbs on top. Serve in the same dish, garnish with parsley and lemon.

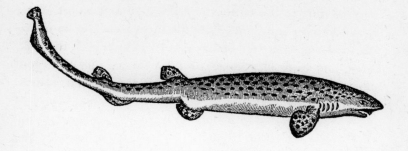

Dog Fish

Edible all the year round, this fish doesn't taste as bad as he looks.

Curried Dog Fish

1 large onion.
1 large apple.
1 large carrot.
2 tomatoes.
Dessertspoonful curry powder.
1 tablespoonful flour.
Cooking oil.
1 oz. sultanas.
Tablespoonful dessicated coconut.
Tablespoonful lemon juice.
$\frac{1}{2}$ pint stock.
Boiled rice.
Dog fish.

Heat the oil and cook the chopped onion until soft. Then add the other vegetables cut up small, and the sultanas, and cook gently until it begins to colour. Sprinkle the curry powder into the mixture and continue to cook for 5 minutes. Make a paste of the flour with some of the stock. Heat the rest of the stock, and add slowly to the paste, stirring all the time. Add this sauce to the ingredients in the pan, and simmer till thickened. Add more stock if necessary. Place half of the curry mixture in the bottom of a fireproof dish or casserole. Cut the cleaned and skinned dog fish into pieces and lay in the dish, and pour the rest of the curry mixture over the top. Cover, and cook in a moderate oven for 45 minutes. Just before serving add the lemon juice and the coconut. Serve with boiled rice.

F. D. FINN'S FAVOURITE RECIPE

Garlic Dog Fish

Boil or poach the dog fish in salted water to which has been added as much crushed garlic as you fancy.

Shad

The twaite shad, and the allice shad are both edible, the allice shad being the better fish. The twaite shad has teeth and has a line of dark spots along its sides. It is caught in rivers and estuaries when it migrates there.

Baked Shad

1 fish.   Salt and pepper.   Butter.

Clean and bone the fish and season it. Soften the butter and spread all over the fish, then place it in a fireproof dish, and bake for 20 minutes. Serve with any savoury sauce.

Fried Shad Roe

Boil the shad roe for 20 minutes in water to which has been added a dessertspoonful of salt and a tablespoonful of vinegar. Drain and plunge in cold water. Drain again and season with pepper and salt, dredge with flour and fry in deep fat until it is golden brown. Serve with fried bacon.

CHAPTER SIX

FISH AND CHIPS BOUILLABAISSE
CHOWDER FISH CAKES
GEFILTE FISH KEDGEREE
FISH PIE TIMBALE
BISQUE ROES
RISOTTO AUX FRUITS DE MER

Fish and Chips

You can fry many fishes, either in steaks or in fillets, dipped in batter, and serve them with potato chips and call it fish and chips: but I am quite unable to give you a recipe which will reproduce the exact and magnificent flavour which is "Fish and Chips". Is it the deep frying oil used again and again until it has a flavour all its own? or is it the flavour of printer's ink from the news-wrapping-paper? or—what is it?

This most delectable English dish has replaced roast beef, or boiled beef and carrots, as our national dish. It needs no seasoning but salt and vinegar, and the drink that goes best with it is a cup of tea!

Fish Pie

1 lb. white fish cooked in court bouillon.	1 lb. mashed potatoes.
	Butter.
½ pint parsley sauce.	Seasoning.
Grated lemon rind.	Browned breadcrumbs.

Flake the fish and mix it with the sauce and seasoning. Place in a greased pie dish and cover with potatoes and dot with butter. Sprinkle crumbs over and bake for 20 minutes in a fairly fast oven.

This is a basic recipe for fish pie, but it can be improved by various additions. Hardboiled egg chopped and added to the parsley sauce. Anchovy sauce added to the white sauce instead of parsley. A tablespoonful of white wine poured over the fish before putting on the potatoes. Or flaky pastry substituted for potatoes.

Roes

Herring Roe Puffs

Rough puff pastry.
Herring roe stuffing (see page 72).

Cut the pastry into strips about ½ inch thick, spread roe stuffing on to half the strips and cover with the other half. Place on a baking tray, brush with egg and cook for 15 minutes.

Boiled Cod's Roe

4 oz. roe per person.
1 dessertspoonful vinegar.
Warm salted water.

Wash the roe and tie it in a muslin bag. Place in warm salted water and add the vinegar. Cook till tender, for about three-quarters of an hour. Drain and serve on toast with lemon parsley butter (see Chapter 7).

Devilled Soft Herring Roes

Butter.	Hot toast.
Made mustard.	Parsley.
Salt and pepper.	Herring roes.

Place two tablespoonfuls of butter in a small pan by the side of the stove, add half a teaspoonful of mustard and the salt and pepper. Melt the butter and add the roes. Simmer gently until the butter be absorbed by the roes. Serve on hot buttered toast, sprinkling with parsley.

"GUIDE TO GOOD FOOD AND WINES" ANDRÉ SIMON *Collins*

Herring Roe Savoury

1 hard roe.	2 oz. butter.
1 soft roe.	$\frac{1}{2}$ teaspoonful salt.
$\frac{1}{2}$ teaspoonful cayenne.	$\frac{1}{2}$ glass white wine.
$\frac{1}{2}$ teaspoonful curry powder.	Chopped parsley.

Place all the ingredients in a saucepan and cook together for 10 minutes, slowly. Then blend thoroughly, if possible in an electric liquidiser. Allow to cool, and serve as a spread, or on biscuits, or in small pastry cases. Wonderful for cocktail parties.

Fritters of Herring Roes

Simmer either soft or hard roes in salted water for 10 minutes. Dry well, then dip in batter and fry in deep fat. Serve with fried parsley and slices of lemon.

"GUIDE TO GOOD FOOD AND WINES" ANDRÉ SIMON *Collins*

Freshwater Bouillabaisse

I think the first and most important fact about a freshwater bouillabaisse is *the more the merrier*. The more mixed the bag, the more intriguing the final flavour. Do not include bream

[108]

or chub, however, unless desperately pressed: the former is mainly slime, the latter mainly bones. But most general sorts of fish may be chucked in. I rate perch and gudgeon at the top —tastier than trout—and you can also add roach, rudd, and dace. Pike are an excellent ingredient, and eels are admirable. To my mind, the perfect ingredients for this dish are perch, gudgeon, pike, and eel (but some connoisseurs dote on carp).

Clean and cut up the fish. You want about a couple of pounds for a decent meal. Cut about half this into small bits, the rest into larger chunks. For the trimmings you'll want a couple of good sized onions, four tomatoes, as much garlic as you can stand, a bay leaf, a pinch of saffron, parsley and fennel, and olive oil.

Slice the onions, peel and pulp the tomatoes. Put the larger, firmer lumps of fish into a pan, and all the vegetable trimmings, and pour in just enough oil to cover the fish. Then pour boiling water over the whole lot and cook fast and furiously for 5 minutes. Take the pan off the heat, and when the mixture has dropped below boiling point, add a generous glass, maybe two, of white wine, and the softer, smaller pieces of fish. Boil the lot for 7 minutes more.

Pour off the liquid into soup bowls, with croutons of fried bread, or pieces of toast. Put the fish flesh into a dish and garnish with the parsley. Serve both at once, the liquid and the flesh, and let joy be unrestrained. Should be consumed with white wine, or stout. The cook, especially, needs a drink, for, as the poet so justly observed,

> A freshwater bouillabaisse
> Includes Dace
> Even if you can't spell it
> You can smell it.

MAURICE WIGGIN'S FAVOURITE FISH RECIPE

Risotto Aux Fruits de Mer

3 or 4 scallops.   1 teaspoonful oil.
1 pint mussels.   Pinch of saffron.
2 or 3 oz. shelled   Bouquet garni.
    shrimps.   2 oz. blanched almonds.
1 cup Patna rice.   1 medium sized onion.
1 cup white stock.   1½ gills dry white wine.
2 oz. butter.   Seasoning.

Garnish 2 hardboiled eggs quartered. Green and
black olives, pinch of paprika.

Wash the scallops well, then poach them in the wine, with
the bouquet garni, seasoning, and a slice of onion. Cook 4 or
5 minutes. Draw aside and allow to cool in the liquor. Wash
the mussels in several waters and remove their beards. Place
them in a large pan, cover well. Shake it over a good heat
until all are open. Strain off the liquor and keep it. Remove
all but half a dozen of the mussels from their shells, leaving the
remaining ones in their shells for the garnish. Keep them hot
by standing them in a colander over hot water. Melt the
butter and oil in a fairly large, strong pan. Add to it the rest
of the onion finely chopped, and soften it without coloration.
Then add the rice and stir it quickly until it is coated with
butter. Heat the stock, add to it the liquor from the mussels
and scallops making it up to rather less than three cupfuls.
Stir in the saffron and pour this on the rice. Now add the
scallops roughly chopped, and the mussels and shrimps, and
almonds. Mix and season well. Cover with a piece of greaseproof paper and the lid and cook in a moderate oven until the
rice is done, without disturbing the rice.

Stone the olives. When the rice is cooked place in a hot

dish to which has been added a spoonful of oil (hot) and rough it up with a fork. Decorate the dish with the eggs, olives, and remaining mussels. Dust with paprika.

Other fish such as oysters, crayfish, or crabs can be added if liked.

"THE IRIS SYRETT COOKERY BOOK" *Faber*

Bisque

Is a fish soup or puree made with any shellfish.

Cook the lobster, or whatever you are using, in white wine court bouillon. When cooked remove from the stove and add a wineglassful of sherry, and leave overnight with the lobster in the liquid. Add 1 lb. of fresh tomatoes and reheat, cooking until tomatoes are soft. Allow to cool again, and then remove the lobster and pound all edible parts and the shell of the body and big claws in a mortar. Then pass this through a fine sieve, and discard what will not go through, putting the sieved fish back into the court bouillon and simmer very gently for 2 hours. Then allow to cool from boiling point and add two beaten egg yolks, a little fresh cream, sherry or brandy to taste, and serve. Season with cayenne pepper and salt. Pass tomatoes through the sieve back into the liquid. The soup can be thickened with a roux made of flour and butter if wished, instead of the yolk of egg.

Gefilte Fish

Can be made with carp, bream, haddock, or mackerel.

3 lb. fish.	Salt, pepper.
2 large onions.	2 slices white bread
2 eggs.	soaked and squeezed.
1 large sliced carrot.	Parsley.
2 stalks celery.	

Skin and bone the fish, keeping the skin intact to use as wrappings. Chop the fish finely, add 1 grated onion, the eggs, salt, pepper, and soaked bread. Make this into neat cakes and use the fish skin to support these. Dice the other onion and the celery and place in the bottom of a saucepan with the fish bones. Then put the fish shapes on top, cover with water, boil quickly, then turn heat low and simmer for $1\frac{1}{2}$ to 2 hours, reducing the liquid by half. Remove from the heat and allow to cool, put the fish shapes on to a separate plate, strain off the liquid and allow to set into a jelly which can be used as a garnish. Also use sliced carrot as a garnish.

"500 DISHES FROM ABROAD" MARGUERITE PATTEN

Fish Chowder

2 lb. cod or fresh haddock.	Dessertspoonful salt.
1 lb. potatoes, cubed.	Pepper.
1 sliced onion.	3 cups scalded milk.
Small piece of	1 tablespoonful butter.
salt pork (2 oz.).	4 dry biscuits.

Clean and skin the fish. Take the head, tail and backbone and put them in a saucepan with pepper and salt and two cups of water. Simmer for 20 minutes, then drain and keep the liquor. Cut the salt pork small and fry until the fat is all out, and cook the chopped onion in this. Then put in the potatoes and two cups of water and boil for 5 minutes, then add the pieces of fish and the liquor from the bones. Simmer for 10 minutes more and add the butter, the milk, and the biscuits, crumbled coarsely.

Fish Cakes

1 lb. cooked fish	1 teaspoonful
(any white fish).	chopped parsley.
1 oz. butter.	1 teaspoonful
1 oz. flour.	anchovy essence.
½ pint milk.	Seasoning.
2 eggs.	Oil.

White breadcrumbs.

Flake the fish and put into a basin with the parsley, and 1 oz. of breadcrumbs. Melt the butter in a saucepan and blend in the flour and then the milk. Season and add the anchovy essence. When boiling stir in one egg yolk. Pour this on to the fish and mix well, and allow it all to get cold. Then taking a piece of the mixture the size of an egg, place on a floured board and shape into a neat cake. Dip into beaten egg and then into fine breadcrumbs, and fry in very hot oil.

The same mixture with the addition of as much cooked potatoes as you like makes the fish go further.

Kedgeree

1 lb. any cold fish (haddock preferred).	2 oz. butter.
	Salt and pepper.
¼ lb. rice.	Cayenne.
2 hardboiled eggs.	

Boil and dry the rice. Divide the fish into flakes, cut up the whites of the eggs, and rub the yolks through a sieve. Melt the butter in a pan and add the ingredients all together. Stir till hot and then turn on to a dish and decorate with the sieved egg yolk which has been kept for this purpose.

Fish Timbale

¾ lb. any white fish.	½ teacupful of shelled shrimps or prawns.
¾ lb. flaky pastry.	
Stale bread.	¼ lb. mushrooms, sliced.
White sauce thickened with cream.	A few oysters if available.

Roll out the pastry to ⅓ inch thick and line a well greased deep cake tin with it. Cut a pastry lid the size of the tin. Line the pastry in the tin with greaseproof paper and put in pieces of bread to prevent sides falling in. Put on the lid lightly and bake in a hot oven for 25 minutes. Remove lid and take out bread and paper. Flake the fish and add to sauce (see Chapter 7) with shrimps, mushrooms, and oysters. Stir all together and cook gently for 10 minutes before putting in pastry case, replacing lid, and heating all together before serving.

CHAPTER SEVEN

SAUCES FOR FISH

Lemon Sauce

$1\frac{1}{2}$ oz. butter.
$1\frac{1}{2}$ oz. flour.
$\frac{1}{4}$ pint thin cream.
1 egg yolk.
$\frac{1}{2}$ pint of the liquid in which the
    fish was cooked.
Seasoning.
Juice of a lemon.
2 tablespoonfuls thick cream.

Heat the butter in a pan and stir in the flour, add the fish stock and thin cream gradually, stirring all the time, and cook until thickened. Whisk in the other ingredients and cook gently for a few minutes longer.

Cheese Sauce

2 cupfuls court bouillon.
2 tablespoonfuls butter.
3 tablespoonfuls flour.
Yolk of two eggs.
$\frac{1}{2}$ cup of cream.
Salt and pepper.
$\frac{1}{2}$ cupful grated cheese.

Reduce the court bouillon by half by boiling. Melt the butter and blend in the flour, then add the court bouillon and cream, stirring constantly. At just below boiling point add the egg yolks, stir well, and add the grated cheese, but do not boil once the egg yolks are in.

[116]

Shrimp Sauce

Shrimps.
1 oz. plain flour.
1 oz. butter.
Pepper and salt.
The liquor and cream in which
the fish cooked.

Melt the butter in a pan and blend in the flour, add the liquor slowly stirring all the time. Season as liked. Add the shrimps and continue to cook slowly until they are heated through.

Sauce Bearnaise

4 oz. butter.
2 egg yolks.
2 tablespoons tarragon vinegar.
1 chopped shallot.
6 peppercorns.
1 tablespoon white stock.
Salt.
1 tablespoon chopped tarragon.

Put the peppercorns, shallot and vinegar into a pan and heat until the vinegar is reduced by half. Then strain, add the stock and the beaten egg yolks. Stand in a double saucepan and heat, whisking all the time, until the mixture thickens. Do not boil. Beat in the butter and the chopped tarragon, and add salt to taste.

Sauce Mayonnaise

1 yolk of egg.
2 tablespoons wine vinegar.
$\frac{1}{2}$ pint olive oil.
$\frac{1}{2}$ teaspoonful French mustard.
Salt and pepper.

Put the mustard in a bowl and add the egg, whisk lightly. Then, whisking all the time, pour in the oil very gradually. Season and add enough vinegar to make the sauce the consistency you like.

Sauce Hollandaise

1 tablespoonful court bouillon.
2 egg yolks.
4 oz. butter.
1 tablespoonful lemon juice.
Pepper.

Heat the court bouillon until reduced by half, add a tablespoonful of water and strain on to the beaten yolks. Heat in a double pan until creamy, whisking all the time. Then whisk in the butter, and add lemon juice and pepper just before serving.

Sweet and Sour Sauce

3 oz. chopped pineapple.
3 oz. pineapple juice.
½ pint water.
Salt.
2 teaspoonfuls oil.
1 tablespoonful soya sauce.
1 tablespoonful Worcestershire sauce.
1 tablespoonful sherry.
2 tablespoonfuls brown sugar.
1 teaspoonful ground ginger.
1 teaspoonful dry mustard.
½ cupful mayonnaise.
2 tablespoonfuls tarragon vinegar.
1 tablespoonful tomato paste.
Pepper.
1 clove garlic or teaspoonful garlic salt.
2 oz. chopped spring or pickled onions.

Put all ingredients except chopped pineapple and onions into a bowl and whisk till blended. Then add the pineapple and onions and heat all together, stirring constantly. Simmer for 10 minutes before use.

A simpler sweet and sour sauce may be made by omitting the sherry, the Worcestershire sauce, the ginger, the mustard and the mayonnaise, and thickening instead with a dessertspoonful of cornflour blended in when mixing.

Sauce Vinaigrette

To three parts of olive oil
    use one part wine vinegar.
Salt.
Pinch of sugar.
Made mustard.
Pepper.

Mix the seasonings with the vinegar, add the oil little by little whisking well all the time.

White Sauce or Sauce Bechamel

1 oz. plain flour.
1 oz. butter.
½ pint milk.
Pepper and salt.

Melt the butter in a saucepan, remove from heat and add the flour, blending well. Return to the heat and cook for a minute or two, stirring all the time. Then add the milk gradually still stirring.

Sauce Tartare

1 hardboiled egg yolk, sieved.	1 raw egg yolk.
½ pint oil.	Salt and pepper.
1 tablespoonful wine vinegar.	Mustard.

1 dessertspoonful each chopped capers and chives.
1 tablespoonful chopped tarragon.

Place the sieved egg in a bowl with the raw yolk. Add the oil very gradually, stirring all the time, then add the vinegar and seasoning, still stirring. Finish with the blanched tarragon, and the chives, and capers.

Maitre d'Hotel Butter

4 oz. butter.
Juice of half a lemon.
2 tablespoonfuls chopped parsley.
Salt and pepper.

Beat the butter until it is creamy then work in the lemon juice and parsley. Season well to taste, and then allow to harden before serving.

Browned Lemon Butter

2 oz. butter.
Squeeze of lemon juice.
Few drops of Worcestershire sauce.

Melt the butter in a pan until it goes brown, then add the lemon juice, sauce, and season to taste.

Mustard Sauce

1 teaspoonful English mustard.
1 teaspoonful French mustard.
2 oz. butter.
1 tablespoonful flour.
1 dessertspoonful vinegar.
2 tablespoonfuls cream or milk.
Salt.
Sugar.
$\frac{1}{2}$ pint milk.

Melt the butter in a saucepan, and stir in the flour and mustard, then the water and vinegar. Add a seasoning of salt and sugar to taste. Rub through a fine strainer or sieve, or blend with a liquidiser, then put back in the saucepan and rewarm, adding the cream or a little milk.

[121]

Beurre de Montpellier

Special sauce for cold fish

> 2 finely chopped shallots.
> Few pieces of watercress.
> 6 leaves of spinach.
> 3 sprigs of tarragon.
> 3 sprigs of thyme.
> 4 oz. butter.
> 1 tablespoonful chopped capers.
> 2 anchovy fillets.
> 2–3 gherkins.
> 2 hardboiled yolks.
> 2 raw yolks.
> 1 gill oil.
> Seasoning.

Put the spinach, the cress and the herbs into boiling water and boil for 3 minutes, then add the shallots. Drain, refresh under cold tap, and drain again. Then squeeze dry in a cloth. Pound in a mortar, or pass through a sieve with the gherkins and capers. Work in the softened butter, and the two sieved hardboiled yolks and the raw yolks. Chop the anchovy fillets as finely as possible and add these. Blend well. Lastly add the oil drop by drop, as for mayonnaise. Season well with pepper and a little salt. Allow to harden before serving.

"THE IRIS SYRETT COOKERY BOOK" *Faber*

INDEX

TO

THE COMPLEAT

ANGLER'S WIFE

INDEX

[125]